Multiple Exposures, Promised Lands

OTHER ESSAYS FROM QUARRY PRESS

Other Voices: Diverse Essays & Stories from the
    Whig-Standard Magazine
edited by ROGER BAINBRIDGE

In Defence of Art: Critical Essays & Reviews
by LOUIS DUDEK

The Crowded Darkness
by DOUGLAS FETHERLING

Some Day Soon: Essays on Canadian Songwriters
by DOUGLAS FETHERLING

The Thinking Heart: Best Canadian Essays
edited by GEORGE GALT

Letters from Managua: Meditations on Politics & Art
by GARY GEDDES

Under the Sun: Occasional Essays
by ALEXANDER SCALA

Powers of Observation: Familiar Essays
by GEORGE WOODCOCK

Anarchism & Anarchists
by GEORGE WOODCOCK

Arguments with the World: Essays by Bronwen Wallace
edited by JOANNE PAGE

Multiple Exposures, Promised Lands

Essays on
Canadian Poetry and Fiction

TOM MARSHALL

Quarry Press

The publisher gratefully acknowledges the support of The Canada Council and the Ontario Arts Council.

Canadian Cataloguing in Publication Data

Marshall, Tom, 1938 –

   Multiple exposures, promised lands: essays on Canadian poetry and fiction

ISBN 1-55082-047-8

1. Canadian fiction (English) — 20th century — History and Criticism. 2. Canadian poetry (English) — 20th century — History and criticism. I. Title.

PS8117.M37 1992   C810'.5409   C92-090447-5
PR9184.6.M37 1992

Cover art by Lawren Harris entitled "Abstraction 1954," reproduced by permission of Margaret H. Knox and Lawren P. Harris.
Design by Keith Abraham.
Typeset by Susan Hannah.
Printed and bound in Canada by Best-Gagné, Toronto, Ontario.

Published by **Quarry Press Inc.**,
P.O. Box 1061, Kingston, Ontario K7L 4Y5.

"It was a double, a multiple exposure!"

A.M. Klein, *The Second Scroll*

Contents

Part Two: Changing Historical News

in memory of
Margaret Laurence and Gwendolyn MacEwen

Foreword

This selection of my writings both formal and familiar — essays and a handful of reviews written over several decades and for a variety of reasons — is necessarily a mixed bag of tricks, containing as it does analyses of texts, more general reflections and commentary on the development of Canadian writing and some of the shapes it has taken (as I see them), some even more general thoughts about poetry and fiction themselves, and (at the other end of my particular spectrum) concrete personal reminiscences of fellow writers, a few of whom have died prematurely.

Some essays arose from my teaching; others have much more to do with my inevitable interest, as a practitioner, in the poems and novels of others (for the purposes of this book, mostly Canadian) both past and present. I cannot be a disinterested observer (if such has ever existed), but I hope that even my most personal and familiar observations will enhance the reader's participation in the writer's (say, Gwendolyn MacEwen's) words and works.

Indeed, in dealing with my own generation, and with contemporaries, acquaintances, and friends of whatever age, I write as a particular human being necessarily caught up in the ongoing process of creation of a Canadian literature. Perhaps I'm laboring the obvious here but I'll say it anyway: if anything gives a degree of unity to *Multiple Exposures, Promised Lands* it must, for better or worse, be my own individual voice, temperament, and sensibility. I'd like to think these particular words (offering some of this, some of that) are one informed person's useful contribution to a continuing national conversation.

1992

Part One
Sounds of Being

1 Sounds of Being

When asked some years ago by interviewer Jon Pearce why I wrote poetry, I said that "one writes to establish what is real, because after all the world is extremely confusing, especially now." The artist retains the child's need to understand, if not to control, the world, to reduce it in scale within the microcosm of his or her art in order to make it somehow more amenable or hospitable. The poet is thus the heir of the shaman, a magician whose function in the tribe is to express mythically the character of vast, mysterious, more or less uncontrollable phenomena like the weather. But the artist is concerned with less external forms of power than the scientist who is the shaman's other heir. Poetry, like all art, deals with inner and outer weather together: in this case, in the medium of words arranged in musical patterns.

Well, this response, published in Jon Pearce's *Twelve Voices* (1980), is very general. I think perhaps I can more concretely express myself if I proceed somewhat more empirically from my reading of important Canadian poems. My "evidence" is work by some major Canadian poets that speaks most eloquently to my own psychic needs.

The great progenitor of a "national" Canadian poetry in the 1960s and afterwards has been Al Purdy. But it is the metaphysics of his nationalism that concerns me here. For Purdy writes (often

in insistent present participles or what somebody once called the
"galloping gerund") of an eternal present, of time as a moving
image of eternity (as Plato, I think, had it). "Transient," which
comes first in his selected poems, *Being Alive* (1978), is one good
example. And in "Roblin's Mills (1)" he declares:

>   Those old ones
>   you can hear them on a rural party line
>   sometimes
>   when the copper wires
>   sing before the number is dialed and
>   then your own words stall some distance
>   from the house you said them in
>   lost in the 4th concession
>   or dimension of wherever
>   what happened still happens

Here, on the magic "party line" that transcends time, in the fourth
concession or dimension of human imagination, the past is also
present, part of what *is*. And in "Roblin's Mills (2)" the party-line
is replaced by the "water eye" of the millpond to suggest once
again the eye of human imagination (or of God?) that "holds"
within itself the past.

In "My Grandfather's Country" Purdy writes:

>   . . . if I must commit myself to love
>   for any one thing
>   it will be here in the red glow
>   where failed farms sink back into earth
>   the clearings join and fences no longer divide
>   where the running animals gather their bodies together
>   and pour themselves upward
>   into the tips of falling leaves
>   with mindless faith that presumes a future

The life-cycle is seen as an endless continuum, finally timeless.
And in "Method For Calling Up Ghosts" he speaks of

the nature of a word being
that when it's been said it will always be said
— a recording exists in the main deep of sound.

Some permanent existence, continuum, process is affirmed by the
imagination and by the very act of poetry. In "Remains of an
Indian Village," possibly my favorite Purdy poem, he writes

> . . . I come here as part of the process
> in the pale morning light,
> thinking what has been thought by no one
> for years of their absence,
> in some way continuing them —
> And I observe the children's shadows
> running in this green light from
> a distant star
> into the near forest —
> wood violets and trilliums of
> a hundred years ago
> blooming and vanishing —
> the villages of the brown people
> toppling and returning —
> What moves and lives
> occupying the same space,
> what touches what touched them
> owes them . . .

The reference to "green light from / a distant star" places the whole
process, "the seasonal cycle and the planet's rhythm," in a cosmic
context of space-time that is ultimately timeless. It is not merely
that the past *lives* and helps to define us now; the act of poetry itself
touches upon an eternal now.

Other major Canadian poets have written of the world's cease-
less flux and of the world's endless birth in human consciousness.
And the new openness of form, the experiments of all kinds that
have been characteristic of Canadian poetry since the 1960s are also,
I believe, expressions of this renewed awareness of larger rhythms.
Concrete poetry, sound poetry, the blurring of the boundaries between

poetry and music, between poetry and graphics, between poetry and prose, the poem-novels (for example, *Beautiful Losers*, *Surfacing*, *Coming Through Slaughter*), the proliferation of longer poems and sequences: all these express a sense of the world's (that is, the universe's) openness and endless self-renewal. We find this large "flow" in key works by our most impressive poets.

A classic example is A.M. Klein's "Portrait of the Poet as Landscape." Of his archetypal poet Klein writes:

> Look, he is
> the nth Adam taking a green inventory
> in world but scarcely uttered, naming, praising,
> the flowering fiats in the meadow, the
> syllabled fur, stars aspirate, the pollen
> whose sweet collision sounds eternally.

This passage suggests that sense-perception is itself creation ("fiat") and that language (the naming and praising of what one perceives) is re-creation ("the/syllabled fur, stars aspirate"), the means by which man participates more fully in God's continuous creation (a notion that probably owes something to Coleridge and his idea of the primary and the secondary imagination). Poetry is celebration of and participation in the constant creation of the universe.

Thus Irving Layton writes of his poet in "The Birth of Tragedy":

> A quiet madman, never far from tears,
>> I lie like a slain thing
>> under the green air the trees
> inhabit, or rest upon a chair
>> towards which the inflammable air
> tumbles on many robins' wings;
>> noting how seasonably
>> leaf and blossom uncurl
> and living things arrange their death,
> while someone from afar off
> blows birthday candles for the world.

The birthday candles signify the way in which the world is continually being reborn both in the poet's imagination and in his re-creation of the process in language. The poet is representative man in his verbal expression of the central action of human consciousness.

In "First" Margaret Avison writes:

> In the mathematics of God
> there are percentages beyond one hundred.
>
> His new creation is
> One, whole, and a
> beginning.

This world is always "One," always whole, and yet always "beginning," always "new" as perceived by the poet (or any consciousness). Similarly, P.K. Page in "Another Space" expresses in terms of "primitive" dance and a "compass rose / surging and altering" the vision of a universe in endless flux yet forever one. (Perhaps, as in D.H. Lawrence's poem "God Is Born," we see that "there is no end to the birth of God.")

In "Animal Syllables," a prose-poem, Gwendolyn MacEwen writes of Toronto Island in these terms:

> The snow-capped coalpiles are a mountain range in Tibet. Sundog the cat enters the house with snow on his eyebrows. All is well with the world. Somewhere out on the breakwater a single gull is preparing for some ultimate flight. Everything begins, everything is a continuum, everything organizes its death. There are red midnights of flowers, there are white midnights of snow. There are no alternatives to pain, there are no alternatives to beauty. The lighthouse describes great cryptic arcs across the darkness. We fold in upon ourselves like the waves, we fold under, falling in and out of the world's vision. How many languages can we know?

"Everything begins, everything is a continuum, everything organizes its death." This echoes Klein, Layton, Avison, Purdy, and Page.

One more example, a passage of prose-poetry from Margaret Atwood's *Surfacing*:

The forest leaps upward, enormous, the way it was
before they cut it, columns of sunlight frozen; the
boulders float, melt, everything is made of water, even
the rocks. In one of the languages there are no nouns,
only verbs held for a longer moment.
The animals have no need for speech, why talk when
you are a word. I lean against a tree, I am a tree leaning.

I break out again in the bright sun and crumple, head
against the ground.
I am not an animal or a tree, I am the thing in which
the trees and animals move and grow, I am a place.

Identification with process and place, with the whole "continuum" of things: this is the shaman's wisdom here in Atwood as in
Purdy before her.

This brings us (as do all my examples) to the question of poet
and environment. Here I speak out of my own experience of func-
tioning as a poet.

A lyric poet's real subject, it seems to me, is always himself or
herself experiencing the world. This determines the form. Form in
poetry is primarily physiological in origin (rhythm and sound-effect
that renders the whole organism, mind and body, experiencing and
responding to the world). This original creative process is itself, of
course, a central action of living, since we all make up the world in
our individual sense-perceptions and memories. Some of us go further to write out of this universal and primary personal creation.
Here language, as a function arising out of the need to communicate primary individual experience and thus create a communal
experience, comes into play.

I have said nothing so far about the notorious problems of language, that most important but also potentially treacherous of
human inventions. Language can certainly be abused and is in any
case a fluid thing in itself. To acknowledge the limitations of language, its trickiness, instability, and inherent difficulties is only
sensible. But some schools of thought seem to exaggerate this
rather obvious insight to the point of absurdity. Genuine poets
attempt patternings of language (through rhythm, sound, image,
denotation, connotations) that may transcend the limitations of

language as a self-enclosed system in order to convey the substantial mystery, complexity, and "feel" of the world. Thus the language of poetry may be dense and multifaceted like dream-language (that cinema of the mind-body in sleep).

Here the ideas of Yury Lotman in *The Structure of the Artistic Text* (1970) and *The Analysis of the Poetic Text* (1972) — as summarized in Terry Eagleton's *Literary Theory* (1983) — seem helpful. Certainly they correspond to my experience. Eagleton paraphrases Lotman thus:

> In poetry, it is the nature of the signifier, the patterns of sound and rhythm set up by the marks on the page themselves, which determines what is signified. A poetic text is "semantically saturated," condensing more "information" than any other discourse; but whereas for modern communication theory in general an increase in "information" leads to a decrease in "communication" (since I cannot "take in" all that you so intensively tell me), this is not so in poetry because of its unique kind of internal organization. Poetry has a minimum of "redundancy" — of those signs which are present in a discourse to facilitate communication rather than convey information — but still manages to produce a richer set of messages than any other form of language.... The literary work continually enrichens and transforms mere dictionary meaning, generating new significances by the clash and condensation of its various "levels." And since any two words whatsoever may be juxtaposed on the basis of some equivalent feature, this possibility is more or less unlimited.

Poetry is that musical use of language — a collaboration, it would seem, of the right and left hemispheres of the brain — that transcends the limitations of language. In this process subject (poet) and object (universe) are not strictly separable: the poet is himself part of the universal flow and (as poet) also its instrument.

Poetry is language at its highest power. It is the language the poet finds both within and beyond the self, the language that is, in his or her physiological processes of sense-perception, the poet's and the world's together, words caught and disposed within that

larger sound and rhythm of things that contains poet and external
landscape and language alike as eternally related parts of its ceaseless continuing. More simply, it is shaped by, even becomes, the
rhythm of the organism (mind and body) interacting with the
rhythm of environment/universe: here metaphor may be important (each poem *is* a metaphor) but it is *sound* that is primary.

Poetry happens at the interface, the flow between inner and
outer worlds.

The most ambitious poetry attempts to capture and contain, or
at least *render, in its very form and flow*, the whole flow of the universe — the larger rhythm of the universe as it "unfolds" in human
consciousness. This is the meaning of artistic form now and in the
past. For example, we no longer believe that iambic pentameter or
heroic couplets (those remnants and expressions of a somewhat
blinkered earlier world-view from the cloister or court) can *or ever
could* — by themselves — adequately render this larger unfolding.
(Strict meter may be mnemonic, but the universal rhythms are not
so neat. David Helwig has suggested to me that the iamb expresses
basic bodily rhythms: breath, heartbeat, walking, making love. I
don't think the same can be said for pentameter.) They can, of
course, still do other, smaller things. But a large poem like, say,
Paradise Lost is now a wonderful museum piece or perhaps a wonderful contraption.

Now, possibly, mid-twentieth-century poetry in Canada and
elsewhere will eventually seem just as archaic (one hopes, *wonderful* and archaic), just as limited, to the people (if there are any)
of future centuries. And it may be that we always fail, relatively
speaking, in the highest endeavor of language. Those who regard
Paradise Lost as a great poem need not feel threatened by my
thoughts about the imperatives of an authentic poetry today.

Still, the greatest poetry, such as that of Dante and Shakespeare,
somehow transcends not only its temporal and philosophical context but even its own governing formal structure. There are mysteries here, obviously, that I cannot pretend fully to understand — but I
suspect that it is not only the great poems' paraphrasable expression
of recognizable and archetypal human experiences that makes them
most durable but also their sheer *sound*, what Eliot, in praising
Walter de la Mare, called "the inexplicable mystery of sound." This

is the pre-verbal base of all poetry. As Robert Frost said, "sound is the gold in the ore." It is sound that expresses that deepest timeless mystery of being in the universe — something that cannot otherwise be "said" at all.

But, to return to the more ordinary fields of history: what can, perhaps, be predicted for the immediate future is that the characteristic dislocation of form in painting, music, and poetry of the age of Einstein, Stravinsky, Picasso, and Ezra Pound will presently resolve itself in a new reintegration or rearrangement of the elements of our consciousness. For a new age as it reveals itself demands and generates a new poetry. In evolving Canada, as Ralph Gustafson has remarked in a preface to the *Penguin Book of Canadian Verse*, we are (as much as any other people) in the thick of that re-creation.

2 A.M. Klein's Poetic Universe

1

O, he who unrolled our culture from his scroll . . .
                "Portrait of the Poet as Landscape"

At first I saw only geometry: triangle consorting with
square, circle rolling in rectangle, the caress parabolic, the
osculations of symmetry: as if out of old time Euclid were
come to repeat his theorems now entirely in terms of
anatomy. Theorems they are, but theorems made flesh. . . .
                Gloss Gimel, *The Second Scroll*

From the above examples, which could easily be multiplied, one
can see that the world of Abraham Klein is very often seen in terms
of a book (or scroll) or as a system of geometry. For he believes with
the Spinoza of his "Out of the Pulver and the Polished Lens" that
the order in the universe can be grasped by the intellect. One can
reduce providence to theorems and set these down in a book; the
book or system of order devised by man (including, of course, any
work of art) is a metaphor for total reality.

There are good reasons for this in Klein's cultural heritage. Jews
do not, like Roman Catholics, venerate images, but they do venerate

the holy scroll itself in its physical aspect. This consists of sheets of parchment sewn together into a scroll rolled at each end onto a piece of wood. In a scroll the Hebrew is copied out letter by letter by hand, and the words must remain exactly as they have been for over two thousand years. The very letters must be preserved, and are venerated as sacred objects.

Hebrew letters are very versatile. They can be used to render numbers (for example, Yod-Aleph for 11), and the pages of the Talmud are numbered in this way. The letter Hai is especially significant since it is used as a short form of the tetragrammaton or four-letter abbreviation of the name of God. Klein concludes *The Second Scroll* with his Gloss Hai, a liturgy affirming the ultimate goodness of God's design.

For Hebrew cabalists letters and numbers have special hidden significances. It seems certain that Klein, who begins a poem "I am no contradictor of Cabala . . .," has been influenced by this sort of mysticism. The idea of Jerusalem as princess (employed in "Yehuda Halevi, His Pilgrimage") and the interpretation of the Song of Songs in terms of spiritual marriage are cabalistic. Safed, a city Klein celebrates in "Greeting on This Day" and *The Second Scroll*, is chiefly noted for the school of cabalistic mystics who flourished there after the expulsion of the Jews from Spain.

According to the *Universal Jewish Encyclopedia* (Volume II), cabala divides itself into speculative cabala, which is the "contemplation of the sensual world as it sprang from the spiritual essence of the Deity," and practical cabala, which is "the Talismanic use of divine names and words for the accomplishment of certain ends." The ultimate goal is the kingdom of the Messiah.

Klein exhibits a concern for "practical" cabala in "Talisman in Seven Shreds." This sonnet sequence employs the legend of the golem or robot created by the rabbi to aid persecuted Jewry. In the legend the golem is brought to life by the placement under his tongue of a piece of parchment bearing the tetragrammaton, but the speaker of Klein's poem mourns the loss of the magic formula.

By way of contrast, we might note that Isaac Luria (1533-72), the chief cabalist of Safed, "invented a whole system of amulets, conjurations, mystic jugglery with words and numbers, and a process of ascetic practices whereby the powers of evil might be overcome."

Cabala was very influential in Poland, the land of Klein's ancestors, after the sixteenth century. Here was founded Chassidism, a
mystical reform movement which aimed at a more direct experience of the divine soul, and here abounded individuals "who, by
manipulating the letters spelling out the Divine Name, were
believed to exercise authority over Spirits." Klein customarily
speaks of illness in terms of possession by defiant evil spirits, and
notes the benevolent presence within himself of his ancestors in
"Psalm XXXVI, a psalm touching genealogy."

Cabala "taught a doctrine of unbroken intercourse between
God and the world." God's creation is matter, but is "ablaze with
soul." God needs to establish His identity: "He is the *En Sof*, the
Endless or Boundless one, who, like Spinoza's substance, cannot
be designated by any known attribute, but who is best called *Ayin*
(Non-existent). Hence in order to make His existence known at
all, the Deity was obliged or wished to reveal Himself to at least
some extent. In other words, He had to become active and creative
in order to make Himself manifest."

God here seems to be motivated by the same need that moti-
vates Klein's poet in "Portrait of the Poet as Landscape." Creation
is self-realization; one must create in order "to be." The poet's
attempt at self-definition through art parallels God's desire to
make himself manifest. More than this, it is an attempt to realize
the godhead innate in every man and is thus an approach to the
Messianic kingdom of the spirit.

Cabala has supported its more extreme doctrines by giving the
letters, words, and names of the Bible special meanings. This can
be done by using the numerical equivalents of the letters, by treat-
ing individual letters as initials or abbreviations of other words, or
by substituting the preceding or following letter of the alphabet.
Klein does not indulge in such extreme verbal jugglery, but his
attempts at a bilingual poetry and the significance he attaches to
alphabetical characters (and to puns and other figures of speech),
can be considered in the light of the cabalistic belief in the magic
properties of language. Klein may not share the literal belief in
magic, but he is certainly influenced by it.

Thus, when he discusses the faith of French-Canadians, it is
natural for him to see a wall-crucifix as an "agonized Y." Similarly,

it is natural for him to think of art as a divine faculty. Michelangelo is for Klein in much more than a trivial sense the Archangel Michael. For the world is One, and art is a kind of communication with the perfect whole. Man collaborates in God's continuous creation. Therefore a connection in language (and, by extension, any connection of any system — whether it be geometry, heraldry, or the law) is a true statement about the whole universe. Seeing creation whole is a matter of partaking in it through the activity of metaphor.

It is useful, after this introduction, to examine the development of those persistent and recurrent metaphors that give to Klein's particular vision of the universe the coherence of myth. We have seen how persistent in his work is the general notion of the universe as God's writ; we may now briefly consider the most important features of the microcosm that is Klein's writ.

The figure that dominates Klein's earliest poetry is certainly the Jew as dwarf or clown and, more important, as martyr and wanderer. The clown is an aspect of the martyr; hunted and persecuted by his enemies, the Jew defends himself by narrowing the scope of his world and by a retreat into self-deprecating humor. "I will dwarf myself," declares Childe Harold, "and live in a hut." This dwarfing process can be seen in the creation of the comic and charming fairy-tale world that takes up most of the latter part of *Hath Not A Jew*. Here is a pleasant diminutive world people by dwarfs, children, homunculi, and elves. Love prevails, and life's problems are scaled down, as in "Bestiary," where a little Jewish boy is able to hunt down the persecuting beast, Nebuchadnezzar, in the pages of the Bible. This poetry is full of the association of the words "little" and "Jew." The little, it seems, can be enough if it is self-contained and self-sustaining, as in "Dr. Dwarf," where all ills are cured by the magic of the Doctor, a sort of diminutive Messiah.

But the Jew is also engaged in a more positive struggle, the journey back to Zion. This journey is for Klein a symbolic representation of each individual's struggle to achieve wholeness within one's self and harmony with the environment. Israel is to be both a physical and a spiritual homecoming for the Jew; the miracle operates on a cultural and a personal level. The goal can be seen in terms of the young poet's love for a beloved woman. She is seen as

the fair princess of chivalry, and the union with her is analogous
to the spiritual marriage of God and his people on their Holy Land.

Because a "Christian" civilization has betrayed the ideals of
chivalry in mistreating the Jews, Klein is able in "Childe Harold's
Pilgrimage" to describe the swastika as "a cross with claws." But he
borrows the conventions of mediaeval chivalry to express his vision
of the quest for Zion that is also the quest for personal integrity.

Both personal love and Zionism are related to the cyclic pattern
of nature. In the activities of love and procreation man exists in
harmony with the purposes of nature. On the land in Israel the
Jewish people can exist as an organic unity in a way that it cannot
in the ghetto of cultural solidarity. Nevertheless, this cultural unity
is also related to the cycle of nature, though at one remove from it.
For it is the symbolic expression of the soul of the people in past
generations and it needs only to be reunited with the land to take on
a new vitality.

Underlying Klein's use of the natural cycle is a concept of the
eternal unchanging order of things. Klein believes in an ultimate
order, in an absolute justice that will ensure Jewry's recovery.
Thus he often employs the figure of the circle, the perfect expression of the world's unity, and speaks in "Out of the Pulver and the
Polished Lens" of the One creation that is contained in God:

> For thou art the world, and I am part thereof;
> he who does violence to me, verily sins against
> the light of day; he is made a deicide.

Man is a part of the One, a fragment praying unto perfection.

As a circle that must periodically re-establish itself as a circle, the
moon is a fit symbol for the fluctuating human power of creativity.
Klein's moon focuses within itself all the welter of human emotions
with which wholeness must be fashioned. The poet of "Business" is
"a hawker of the moon," and Klein speaks in "Preface" of poetic fame
as a matter of setting one's thumbprint on the moon. The moon is
identified with an amazing variety of objects — charming or grand or
sinister — in Klein's early poetry. It is usually an indicator of his
mood and the focus of his poetic universe.

In "Greeting on This Day" terrified Jews "see the moon drip

gore." In "Design for Mediaeval Tapestry" the moon is "a rude gargoyle in the sky" of a Christian and Judaeophobic world. But in "Out of the Pulver and the Polished Lens" the moon is God's "little finger's fingernail," and in "Haggadah" it is a golden platter in the sky.

In "Letters to One Absent" the moon is a mirror in which lovers find each other, and in "Psalm XXI" it is the seal of God upon his open writ; it appears to be the creative lens for both God and man, that area of the soul in which man and God are joined. The force that enables man to love and to create works of art analogous to God's creation is the God within him. The moon may then be said to function in Klein's early poetry as a symbolic expression of the creative world-soul.

It is significant, then, that in the time of his greatest disillusionment and doubt about the nature of the order in the universe Klein's moon becomes a "smooth hydraulic dynamo." For the poetry of the middle and late 1930s suggests that if there is a God man has no meaningful contact with him. The tetragrammaton, the talisman that once enabled man to exercise the creative power of the God within, has been shredded and has lost its efficacy.

The figure that dominates this poetry is the golem or mechanical man. In this perfectly mechanical and materialistic age, the poet, who represents creative man, has become obsolete. In "Barricade Smith: His Speeches," which contains the image of the hydraulic moon, the poet is caricatured as a fool wasting his energies on "stars archaic and obsolete dew."

In "Manuscript: Thirteenth Century" Klein's fair princess, once the symbolic expression of love's fulfillment, gives herself to a villain and is brought to ruin, and in "Barricade Smith: His Speeches" she is demoted to debutante. Barricade Smith, like a true knight, loves her "from afar," but she marries first "the tenth cousin of the Czar" and then a "closer relative of a deposed king," whom she eventually divorces and gives two million dollars as "a little tip."

The poetry of the early 1940s, however, expresses the recovery from this disillusionment in a reassertion of the figures that dominated the earliest poetry. The Jew as wanderer or spiritual seeker, the fair princess, the Utopian land of Israel, the moon-mirror, and the natural cycle are all restored to their original significances.

There are changes and new features, however. The notion of a cosmic court of law by which Jewry's enemies are to be condemned is introduced in order to suggest the justice that must ultimately prevail in the universe. Related to this is the curious fact that the comic dwarf and the mindless golem (or automaton) seem now to be combined in Hitler, the arch-villain and chief disruptive influence in Klein's universe. What had seemed mechanical and inhuman is not, it appears, of any ultimate significance. Hitler is nothing more than a frustrated little man on the rampage, even though the restoration of harmony in Klein's universe is now dependent upon his destruction.

It is interesting that Klein now refuses to see the Jew as a comic dwarf. The Jew as martyr and seeker after perfection has eclipsed the Jew as clown, and the godlike Uncle Melech is lurking in the wings.

In the poem "Autobiographical" (1943), which seems to mark the midpoint of Klein's development, the poet's personal quest for the "fabled city" of innocence and security foreshadows the career of Uncle Melech, but the city sought by this particular wandering Jew is not the actual Jerusalem (or even Safed); it is the enchanted Montreal of his childhood. This realization leads us inevitably to the truth that any city can be a fabled city, that each individual has a personal Zion of the imagination.

This notion, which was at least implicit in Klein's earlier poetry, now brings him to the exploration of the Canadian scene that dominates the poetry of the late forties. This study of Canada provides another opportunity to express his view of man's place in the universe. The belief in man's divine creativity, his ability to unite himself to other men and even to God through self-expression, underlies the experiments in a bilingual poetry. Language is a substantial magic that can unite men in sympathy.

In the poetry of the "Canadian" period the figure of the dwarf-clown is found again, but he is not now a villain or a specifically Jewish hero. He is Everyman. He is individual man as a minority of one — as martyr and clown and wanderer and hero combined. He is the beleaguered and yet comical French-Canadian of "Political Meeting," the Indian in his "grassy ghetto," the lone bather immersed in animal delight, the isolated poet, and, finally, the "nth Adam," who is not only the poet but every man with the creative power of God lying dormant in him.

Because Klein is feeling his way into the problems of a Christian society in his French-Canadian poems, he now gives to Christian symbols a more positive significance than he once did. This is, of course, a necessary consequence of the belief that Montreal may be as much a fabled city as Safed. Man's hopes can be centered upon the Oratoire de St. Joseph as well as Safed, or, more practically, upon a grain elevator. Klein's discovery of his favorite middle-eastern landscape in the "Josephdream" of the grain elevator signifies his realization that Utopia might be anywhere, though it is probably in Israel for the Jew. This enables us to see the Utopian Israel of *The Second Scroll* as a symbolic expression of every man's imagined home.

In this poetry we lose sight of the beautiful princess. Love is presented as a memory, a remembered magic at the top of Mount Royal. The creative moon, too, has vanished (though it reappears in *The Second Scroll* which concludes with "new moons, festivals and set times"). But the figure of the circle remains very prominent. We find (in "Portrait of the Poet as Landscape") "the mirroring lenses forgotten on a brow," and the poet wearing his zero as an ambiguous garland; we find both the natural cycle and its cultural equivalent in the movement of the rocking chair and the Anjou ballad.

For the first time water becomes very important. Since the sea is a traditional symbol for birth and renewal, it is curious that Klein, who was always concerned with various kinds of resurrection, did not use it before. In *The Rocking Chair* he does so in order to suggest both the neglected state of the submerged poet and the birth of a shining new world in his imagination. The poet's submersion can be (like the cultural ghetto of the Jew) a kind of protection. It offers the comfort every man may take from the exercise of his imagination, and provides a home in the private world of memories and hopes. Klein writes in "Lookout: Mount Royal" of

> the photographer's tripod and his sudden faces
> buoyed up by water on his magnet caught
> still smiling as if under water still . . .

The deep well of memories, instincts, and creative impulses can become one with the creative lens; thus, water serves the function the moon served in the early poetry.

The suggestion is that man can express his personal experience of the universe in the work of art, a distinct and communicable microcosm. In *The Rocking Chair* Klein re-creates childhood memories; in "And in That Drowning Instant" he submerges himself once again in racial and cultural memories, but surfaces, so to speak, in the re-creation of the experience as poetry.

In the poetry of *The Rocking Chair* geometry tends to replace law as the system used to suggest the ultimate order of the universe. This is a subtler way of expressing faith in the stability and unity of creation since it is less dependent than law upon human notions of morality. The further suggestion of the use of the alphabet and of scroll imagery is that the universe may contain a message from God.

Man's organized perception can at least approximate God's creativity. In "Krieghoff: Calligrammes" the artist employs a magic language to communicate with God, to participate in His creation. By ordering the "blank whiteness" of his experience he enables himself and his world to be known.

This brings us back to the solitary man who is Everyman. In *The Second Scroll* we find a protagonist, Uncle Melech, who, as the successor to Childe Harold, Solomon Warshawer, and Yehuda Halevi, is the wandering Jew, and, thus, Jewry itself. He is also Abraham Klein. And beyond this he is the creative man, and, thus, the Messiah. For the Messiah can finally be identified as the creative man who seeks and discovers God in himself.

Klein's chief heroes — Spinoza, Yehuda Halevi, Euclid, Michelangelo — have always been creative men reaching to God and attempting to establish His order. Man is the nth Adam, a solitary individual whose task is that of every individual before him — to perceive and express and thus re-create the universe in order to define it as a context for himself. The God within, the lens, must attempt to focus in itself the whole of the God without. All self-expression — whether it results in a system of geometry, the Anjou ballad, a rocking chair, a Hebrew brand-name, or the Sistine Chapel — is a means to this end.

Klein's own interpretation of the Sistine paintings is an exercise of language as magic. The ceiling is seen as geometry and expressed in language that vividly re-creates its physical presence at the same time as it describes the glory and the dangerous limitation that is the human condition. Man is depicted by Michelangelo ("say rather the Archangel Michael") as a potential god caught in the perilous wheels that seem to determine suffering and death. He is able to achieve divinity in an art that may communicate its infinite meaning to individuals of succeeding generations. Klein contends:

> It well may be that Michelangelo had other paradigms in mind: there is much talk of Zimzum and retraction; but such is the nature of art that though the artist entertain fixedly but one intention and one meaning, that creation once accomplished beneath his hand, now no longer merely his own attribute, but Inspiration's very substance and entity, proliferates with significances by him not conceived or imagined. Such art is eternal and to every generation speaks with fresh coeval timeliness. In vain did Buonarotti seek to confine himself to the hermeneutics of his age; the Spirit intruded and lo! on that ceiling appeared the narrative of things to come, which came indeed, and behold above me the parable of my days.

Melech-Klein finds in the ceiling a prophecy both of the Jewish suffering of the twentieth century and of the Messianic era that is to follow. Here we certainly have art as a communication with God.

Klein's own art in Gloss Gimel involves the creation of a rich prose heightened by effects of sound, rhythm, sensual imagery, and metaphor to the power of poetry, a language like that he employed in parts of "Out of the Pulver and the Polished Lens." With "Portrait of the Poet as Landscape," these are surely his most powerful and moving performances. Few English poets of the twentieth century have been capable of such sustained and concentrated and controlled passion. But then, few modern poets have retained the kind of belief in man (and, as feminists may well note, it seems to be specifically *man*) and in God that would enable them to see their own utterance as fiat.

2

For them, for them the world lacks symmetry!
"Les Filles Majeures"

And now in imagination he has climbed
another planet, the better to look
with single camera view upon this earth —
"Portrait of the Poet as Landscape"

O love which moves the stars and factories . . .
"Annual Banquet: Chambre de Commerce"

A.M. Klein's gift for caricature has frequently been remarked upon by his critics. I myself wrote once that Klein had created in the latter part of *Hath Not A Jew* "a pleasant diminutive world peopled by dwarfs, children, homunculi and elves" where "life's problems are scaled down" to manageable proportions. John Sutherland had taken, however, a dimmer view of the matter, remarking that "the real world is made an excuse for escaping into a world of romance" and that "people and their tragedies are dissolved by the childlike fancy playing over them." Sutherland admired Klein's art of caricature, especially in a poem like "Elijah":

> Wished he, he could gather
> The stars from the skies,
> And juggle them like marbles
> Before our very eyes. . . .

but felt that such art was escapist and sentimental. In *The Rocking Chair*, however, Sutherland found a new blend of toughmindedness and good humor in poems like "Political Meeting," with its caricature of Montreal's wartime mayor Camillien Houde, and in the portraits of the lonely and paranoid Canadian poets. And it is easy to demonstrate that caricature need not evade or defeat social and cultural criticism. I don't think it comes off when Klein attempts to make a dwarf of Hitler in *The Hitleriad*, perhaps because hatred untempered by magnanimity or pity or understanding has a natural tendency to *magnify* its object, but familiarity with his characters — his comic rabbis, French-Canadians, and poets — breeds an engaging mixture of affection and sharp observation.

In these instances Klein is concerned with "little" people, with those attempting more or less adequately to cope with the complexities and cruelties of a world beyond their complete understanding. (I am not sure to which of her "victim positions" Margaret Atwood would assign these particular protagonists, but I prefer, in any case, to use other terms of reference, though hers are more or less accurate, as far as they go. Ms. Atwood was not, as her generous acknowledgement to earlier writers suggests, the first person to apply the key word "survival" to the experience of Canadian literature, and most of us, I suspect, have our own list of such words: survival, garrison, communication, identity, etc. The one most relevant to the concerns of this essay is "perspective," and probably it was an older poet, Margaret Avison, who fixed it in my mind.)

To reduce the world to size in the lens of the imagination is to alter one's perspective, one's consciousness. It is not to overcome or to control the world (nor do the frantic power-struggles between individuals and groups disappear), but it is to come to imaginative terms with the world, to live creatively in the face of cruelty and complexity. Such an art affirms the autonomy and even the gaiety of the human mind. It may be that it "makes nothing happen" outside the mind, but herein perhaps lies (paradoxically) its greatest usefulness.

A shifting perspective can render (and alleviate) our sense of smallness within the Canadian physical vastness. In a fashion similar to Klein, Stephen Leacock had presented Mariposa, even the Mariposa Belle, as Canada in miniature, a small place whose pretensions and fantasies and vices are comic because ineffectual, and whose real values are imposed by a lucky smallness. Leacock too shifts easily from comedy to pathos, and it could be said that his microcosmic lens domesticates tragedy.

There are, of course, notable foreign examples of this sort of thing. One thinks of Emily Dickinson, a marvelous miniaturist, who reduces Death and locomotives to size with her flippant and ironic wit, and of the great master of satiric comedy, Jonathan Swift. It was he after all who first exposed his gullible Everyman to

a race of physical and moral pygmies rather like the English, and
then turned the tables on him by surrounding him with giants who
are able to regard him with friendly contempt and to dismiss his
"enlightened" civilization as "the most pernicious race of little odi-
ous vermin that nature ever suffered to crawl upon the surface of
the earth." Here, the shift in perspective has taken in the reader,
too, since the reader was able to laugh at *others* in the first instance
and is then included in the general condemnation of the second.
Gulliver's consciousness undergoes alteration, and he observes:

> I reflected what a mortification it must prove to me to
> appear as inconsiderable in this nation as one single
> Lilliputian would be among us. . . . It might have pleased
> fortune to let the Lilliputians find some nation, where the
> people were as diminutive with respect to them, as they
> were to me. And who knows but that even this prodigious
> race of mortals might be equally overmatched in some
> distant part of the world, whereof we have yet no discovery?

Of course, the "size of things" for the imaginative individual
depends, once again, upon one's mental perspective.

I've suggested elsewhere in an essay on Stephen Leacock that a
shifting perspective is appropriate to the Canadian social and physical reality. The effect need not be comic, and indeed, as the above
examples indicate, different sorts of comic or satiric effect may be
developed. In the poems of Irving Layton the poet's identification
with insects on the one hand and gods and giants on the other can
be comic and serious at once. (Here, the word is "ambivalence,"
though Layton had another way of putting it when he spoke of "an
ironic balance of tensions.") And in Earle Birney's poems "Slug in
Woods" and "David" the shift in perspective is tragic. Near the
close of "David" the unfortunate narrator, Bobby, "squelches" a slug
as he flees from the corpse of the friend he has had to kill. In "Slug
in Woods" Birney had given us a slug's-eye view, and in "David"
two boys climb mountains to achieve something like a god's-eye
view. The imagery suggests that they are climbing to the sun, like
Icarus. (One thinks here of David Canaan in *The Mountain and the
Valley*. And of all those poets — Roberts, D.C. Scott, Frank Scott on

Ararat — who have wanted this long large perspective.) But in "David" (as in *The Mountain and the Valley*) the god's-eye view turns out to be a slug's-eye view after all. "As flies to wanton boys are we to the gods, they kill us for their sport."

If there is humor, or at least "sport," involved here, it is a grim humor indeed, like the jesting of Margaret Laurence's malicious, chuckling god. Such a view of things is at the other pole from the general optimism of Irving Layton.

In his use of caricature and of the ironic, shifting perspective Klein is closer to Layton and Leacock than to Birney. Bitterness is kept in its place. For in Klein's best work there is always a geniality that balances his intense awareness of injustice and of human suffering. He sympathizes deeply with most of his not-so-beautiful losers — the poets, Indians, Jews, librarians, habitants, filles majeures, hustlers, politicians, and harassed businessmen of *The Rocking Chair* — and at the same time all are placed within the grand context of a divine (and human) comedy, the ongoing process of natural and human life. If, for the individual, the world "lacks symmetry," a sense of balance may be restored by the poet's (or, more generally and democratically, the human imagination's) shift to the transcendent perspective of "another planet." The ego dissolves, and another, more profound identity emerges. Insofar as the reader experiences this, the reader has resurrected Klein's drowned poet. The conclusion of "Portrait of the Poet as Landscape" then becomes triumphant; it is no longer ambiguous. The doors of perception are cleansed, and the world is seen as continual rebirth, wonder, and delight (as in Klein's "Snowshoers," Layton's "The Birth of Tragedy," and Avison's "Snow" — in two of these cases, as I think Atwood pointed out, winter and whiteness are seen as wonderful instead of being merely sterile and threatening: here the word "survival" *is* involved, and it is the soul's survival that is, in a very immediate sense, at stake). Klein continues to say to us: go beyond your self-imposed caricatures (having recognized them as such, and laughed at them), go beyond your mental "sets," your social and personal self-images; lose them, lose your mind even, lose your identity, and then you may find it.

1973

3

Gretl Fischer's study of A.M. Klein's religious thought, *In Search of Jerusalem*, has been much criticized by reviewers to the neglect, it seems to me, of its very solid virtues. Not that this was altogether unpredictable. I find, on consulting my own quite favorable reader's report on her manuscript, that I too noted even before publication that Mrs. Fischer was much less concerned with the quality of Klein's work than with the philosophy it might reveal, and went on to remark that surely Klein's chief value to us in future would have to do with the quality of his best work and its place in the development of a distinctive Canadian literature and culture. But most of my remarks were admiring, and for this reason: Mrs. Fischer's book illuminates more than anything else written about Klein the difficult question of just what and with what firmness and consistency he believed about the culture and religious tradition within which he lived. The emphasis on the poet's interest in cabala, Chassidism, and Spinoza's philosophy seems to me to be a very necessary corrective to those commentaries which stress the importance of the more orthodox Talmudic tradition to the neglect of other aspects of the Jewish heritage, or which go to the other extreme in attempting to transform Klein into a "secular humanist" without deep religious conviction. Klein's social concern was not finally a rejection of his religious belief but part of it. Mrs. Fischer seems to me to be almost certainly correct in her argument that Klein abandoned a narrow orthodoxy in order to pursue a broader religious vision that would illuminate both past and present, both the people Israel and the new Jerusalem of Canada. That he succumbed to illness and silence anyhow is tragic; but he ran the risks that — in the face of history — all Utopian visionaries run.

Klein the man, mysterious though he was, comes a little more into focus in Seymour Mayne's collection of essays and other materials, *The A.M. Klein Symposium*. This publication, a record of the sessions held at the University of Ottawa in May 1974, is, like the special number of *Jewish Dialog* (Passover, 1973), a useful supplement to Mrs. Fischer's and Miriam Waddington's studies and — because of its historical interest — a useful addition to my own

A.M. Klein (1970), which collected reviews and articles on the poet's work throughout his creative life and afterwards. Especially interesting in this regard are Klein's own letters, printed or excerpted here, to his McGill friends A.J.M. Smith and Leon Edel. These cast light upon the esoteric details and design of certain poems (for example, "Autobiographical") and of *The Second Scroll*. Klein's grave, somewhat ponderous and ornate wit (and perhaps also a certain prescience) is in evidence when he writes to Smith about the latter's anthology: "A thousand thanks for your Indian poems. They are idea-provoking. Perhaps what we need in Canada is a little interlude of primitivism." Or when he speaks of Northrop Frye's "pontifical irrelevancies." Or when he praises his friend thus: "For hotel-registers to the contrary notwithstanding, not everybody is Smith" (a not quite private joke that finds its way into "Portrait of the Poet as Landscape").

Leon Edel's paper on *The Second Scroll* is eloquent in praise but judicious; Gretl Fischer's paper, like her book, makes good sense of Klein's abiding interest in Spinozan philosophy and cabala, and Phyllis Gotlieb's paper deals engagingly with the importance of Chassidism in the poems and *The Second Scroll*; Usher Caplan provides a description of the Klein papers in the National Archives and a more complete bibliography than we have had before; Marya Fiamengo offers an ingenious account of the "Catholic resonances" in Klein's poems; and M.W. Steinberg writes well of Klein's achievement and of the intermingling of influences and cultures that makes his work so distinctive.

Still, it is impossible for me not to remark that the occasion itself was much more exciting and moving than this record. (Ralph Gustafson's account gives the reader some inkling of this.) There were as many poets, critics, and teachers in the audience as there were on the program. To put such notable Canadians as Leon Edel, Leo Kennedy, Irving Layton, P.K. Page, D.G. Jones, Elizabeth Brewster, Ralph Gustafson, Stuart MacKinnon, Guy Sylvestre, Louis Dudek, Dorothy Livesay, F.R. Scott, A.J.M. Smith, and David and Sophie Lewis into a series of rooms together is to guarantee fireworks. Lewis was about to bring the federal government (and as it happened in the subsequent election, himself) down that week, but spent a good part of Sunday afternoon engaged in public verbal

battle over the meaning of Klein's long silence with the equally
rhetorical and forceful Irving Layton. Those of us who were also on
this panel were, not altogether unhappily, reduced to the status of
spectators at an old family quarrel by these gifted actors. It's a pity
that we don't have here a transcript of that exchange — I believe it
exists on tape — since it revealed two quite distinct attitudes to the
Montreal Jewish community for which Klein was a spokesman and
against which Layton has long been in rebellion.

1977

4

My grandfathers were both scholarly men in Europe. One,
when he came to Canada and settled in Winnipeg before the
First World War, remained wedded to his past; his relatives
proceeded to make their fortunes while he worked for
community institutions and maintained his righteous
poverty. The other, who came later, found his way into the
garment business and eventually did well enough to move
his family into Rosedale before he died at an early age.

Basically, those were the choices: either to cling to the old
ways and treat the new world as an opportunity to sustain a
traditionally Jewish life without threat of attack; or to cast
off what was cumbersome about the past and accept
Canada's invitation to achieve success. Most chose the latter
approach; those who didn't saw their children do so. The
sense of inevitability that characterized this transformation
of Jewish life made the process seem almost preordained.
There was something, indeed, in the notion of this being the
Promised Land; and if not the Promised Land, then at least it
was the land of promise.

This passage from Mark Sarner's essay "Beyond the Candles of
Chanukah" makes a point that is made over and over again in the
anthology *The Spice Box*. The Jewish experience in Canada is one
in which the old ways have been gradually eroded. The life of A.M.

Klein, Canada's first Jewish writer of real importance, is exemplary here.

It has often been observed that Canada's Jews have made a cultural contribution far out of proportion to their numbers in the general population. In particular, such writers as Klein, Irving Layton, Mordecai Richler, Adele Wiseman, Leonard Cohen, Miriam Waddington, Eli Mandel, Matt Cohen, and others have enriched Canadian literature greatly. However, *The Spice Box* does not always present each of its thirty-seven authors at his or her best. Editors Morris Wolfe and Gerri Sinclair seem concerned to demonstrate sociological insight and Jewish content rather more than the highest aesthetic achievement. Thus, one gets interesting poems from Klein, Layton, and Cohen but not their very best work. And an excerpt from Wiseman's *Crackpot* cannot really convey the power of her writing in that novel and in *The Sacrifice*. One needs the cumulative effect of her style and structure for that.

The short stories in this collection are more successful in entertaining as well as instructing. Ted Allan's "Lies My Father Told Me," the sentimental tale of a grandfather, a boy, and an old horse, retains its charm. Jack Ludwig's "A Woman of Her Age" poignantly presents the changes that new wealth brings to an old woman formerly of Montreal's ghetto. Matt Cohen's "The Watchmaker" unfolds obliquely a tale of the Holocaust. Richler's "Mortimer Griffin, Shalinsky and How They Settled the Jewish Question" is the hilarious story that foreshadowed his novel *Cocksure*. Helen Weinzweig's "Hold That Tiger" is an effective Kafkaesque fable. But my favorite story is David Lewis Stein's "Fresh Disasters," a powerful and moving account of political and personal frustration as the 1960s pass into history.

There is much of interest in this book about the immigrant experience, the old world and the new, the Holocaust. There is not a great deal about Israel. More important are the Jewish worlds of the Prairies, Winnipeg, Toronto and (especially) Montreal. Here Klein flourished for a time but also underwent the tensions that eventually brought him to a breakdown and a long silence.

Like One That Dreamed is the first biography of A.M. Klein. In it Usher Caplan's account of the poet's life is supplemented by photographs and by excerpts from Klein's poems, his unpublished, somewhat autobiographical fictions, and his notebooks. Though Klein was one of the most conservative and least "bohemian" poets who ever lived, his life is nevertheless fascinating and moving, partly because of the rich but already vanishing immigrant Jewish world from which he emerged and partly because of his mysterious breakdown. Canadian poets — E.J. Pratt, D.C. and F.R. Scott, Earle Birney, Layton, Al Purdy, Dorothy Livesay, Miriam Waddington, P.K. Page, etc. — are generally a hardy, long-lived lot of survivors (especially when set beside their more suicidal or breakdown-prone American contemporaries); Klein is the one tragic hero of Canadian poetry.

Usher Caplan writes: "The gradual break-up of the immigrant community, occurring at the same time in many other North American cities as well, had cultural implications for Klein of which he was painfully aware." His early writings seemed to have less and less relevance to the new urban world that replaced the old one. Klein's creative solution to this problem was to address himself first to the world of French Canada and then to the renewal of the Jewish people in the State of Israel. By locating his Promised Land both in Canada and in Israel he produced his finest books, *The Rocking Chair* and *The Second Scroll*.

But at the height of his literary achievement in the 1950s Klein suffered from depression, attempted suicide, underwent treatment for a time, and eventually retired into a silence that lasted till his death in 1972. Caplan tells this story with great tact, giving the facts but refusing to indulge in any extravagant speculation about ultimate causes. It seems clear that Klein took on more than he, an extremely sensitive and proud man, could handle: an exhausting schedule of fund-raising speeches for Israel; much debilitating hackwork for Samuel Bronfman; a mind-bending word-by-word commentary on Joyce's *Ulysses*; an abortive and humiliating political career; a burden of intense anxiety about the Holocaust, continued anti-semitism in Soviet Europe, and the Bomb; and even a sense of literary failure when manuscripts were rejected and a play failed in New York.

Klein's father, like one of Mark Sarner's grandfathers, chose to remain unworldly and in "righteous poverty" in the new world. Klein himself wanted to make it as poet, as community worker, and as a public figure. If he was not really well suited to the last role, he is still one of Canada's two or three most important poets writing in English. Caplan's fine biography can only add to our understanding of the complex man behind the poems.

1983

5

A.M. Klein's *Short Stories* poses a special problem for the reviewer who is already on record with the judgment that Klein is one of the three or four finest poets that English Canada has known. As a prose writer he has been known only for his passionate poetic novel *The Second Scroll* — a response to the Holocaust that antedates D.M. Thomas's *The White Hotel*, another poet's novel, by some thirty years. Now Klein's collected shorter fiction offers us a few hits, some near-misses, and a number of embarrassing or immature sketches that might perhaps better have been left interred in old journals. These pieces are, with significant exceptions, more interesting to the serious Klein scholar (who will find Professor Steinberg's informative introduction and notes very useful) than to the general reader or the critic in search of excellence. But then Klein the poet also left us a good deal of undistinguished, mannered, and overblown work. It is his finest poems, especially those in *The Rocking Chair* (1948), that matter.

Klein's fictional bent seems to have been in the direction of the metaphysical and the fantastic. His fables and parables (for these are not "stories" in the sense that admirers of Alice Munro, Clark Blaise, Joyce Marshall, or Mavis Gallant might use the word) are populated by ghetto eccentrics: half-wits, talking birds, dwarfs, fairies (like Jews and poets an endangered species in the modern technological world), giants, devils, Siamese twins and other physical grotesques, spies, beggars, hangmen, and prisoners. As in his poetry Klein's focus shifts as time goes on from fairy tales and charming anecdotes of the ghetto to social and political fables of the 1930s and afterwards. Some of the later pieces are surreal and Kafkaesque; there is a flavor of anti-communism and of the world after the war about these. The best "fictions" are intellectual and philosophical in their appeal like those of Borges and Nabokov, two other multilingual poets with highly metaphysical concerns.

Unfortunately, Klein's wit, his playfulness of style and language, can be ponderous, ornate, and offputting in a way that Borges and Nabokov (and their common forerunner Joyce) usually know how to avoid. And some pieces are didactic in a heavy-handed way. In others (for example, "A Myriad-Minded Man") a sometimes delightful linguistic exuberance overwhelms any serious point or narrative development. Some readers may nevertheless enjoy, as I do, the *flavor* of such sketches.

And there are some notable successes. Some of the ghetto sketches and tales (such as "The Seventh Scroll") are interesting slices of life. "Friends, Romans, Hungrymen" is a weirdly effective fable about unemployment. "And the Mome Raths Outgrabe" wittily describes an international conference whose delegates come to blows over Freudian, Marxist, and other interpretations of Lewis Carroll's "Jabberwocky": this was written long before *The Pooh Perplex* and before the arrival of such current jargon-ridden critical fads as post-structuralism and deconstructionism, but it can serve as commentary on them. A more sombre piece, "Letter From Afar," has as its premise the notion that the prominent victims of Stalin's purges were not executed but lived on in a remote part of the Soviet Union as a reward for having confessed and played their parts in the show trials. Klein explores here the paranoid psychology of a totalitarian regime.

Anti-communism also informs his finest fiction, "The Bells of Sober Spasitula," in which a Russian composer becomes a victim of the Revolution. Through his experience Klein illuminates the modern experience of exile, the relationship of the artist to ideology (whether Christian or Marxist), and the relationship of the ideal and the material, the spiritual and the carnal, in the creation of art. This is Klein's subtlest and most resonant fable apart from *The Second Scroll*. The book is worth having for this piece alone.

Who knows? If "The Bells" had been published when it was written, and if Klein had not fallen silent in the 1950s, then perhaps the author of *The Second Scroll* might have blossomed anew as a Montreal South American, one of the new fabulists of the novel.

1983

3 E.J. Pratt's Good Sense

1

I never thought that E.J. Pratt and I had anything much in common beyond being poets and professors of English literature with an interest in history. Now I discover that his first versifications were "schoolboy lampoons on his teachers" for the amusement of his classmates. I believe some of my own lampoons (such as the one that likened my grade six teacher to Walt Kelly's Albert the Alligator) still exist in one of my more ancient files. It makes me wonder how many other Canadian poets began in this essentially social fashion.

E.J. Pratt on His Life and Poetry is a very useful book for the serious student of Pratt. For other readers it will, I suspect, be only intermittently interesting. It is often very repetitive, since Pratt's favorite sayings, phrases, and anecdotes were trotted out over and over again in his comments on his life and work; and in stretches it is downright boring. Editor Susan Gingell attempts in her introduction to refute the assertion of Louis Dudek and Michael Gnarowski that there was "almost no developed literary theory from E.J. Pratt," but in my judgment Dudek and Gnarowski are correct. Still, this book is quite illuminating about Pratt's methods.

It confirms among other things that Pratt was very much a poet of fact (with salutary flights into fantasy), a man very much concerned to get right and then to versify those details of science, technology, and heroic animal and human struggle that "took hold" of him and fired his imagination. He was suspicious of a more introspective poetry: "If poetry just meant warbling, or just spinning fancies out of one's inner consciousness, there would be some force in the question [of whether poetry should be tied to humdrum fact]. A bird does the first; a spider the second." (It is worth noting here that Al Purdy has compared himself as poet to a spider who spins from himself webs to support his own existence.) The only Canadian poet here commended (or even mentioned) by Pratt is Earle Birney, his obvious successor as poet of fact (as Purdy is Birney's successor).

Pratt goes so far as to speak of the "task of beating a group of facts and impressions into verse." (It is only fair, I suppose, to allow that he, a playful speaker, may have been using the word "beating" somewhat facetiously. But the notion of poetic process suggested here is surely a rather naive one.) Pratt learned early that his poetry had to be made out of the concrete and the material; in this respect he departs from late-Victorian poetry just as much as the "imagist" Ezra Pound. His commentaries on particular poems offer much data about seals, whales, whaling then and now (without, curiously, any reference to *Moby Dick*), disasters and adventures at sea, and other matters that he attempted to transform into poetry.

It is interesting at one point to overhear Pratt waxing enthusiastic about the "world attention" accorded to the heroic rescue operation of Fried, the captain of the *Roosevelt* who became an "international figure" in the late 1920s. For who remembers Fried today? I suppose the gung-ho astronauts of *The Right Stuff* have replaced naval heroes of the past in the popular imagination, though the fame of Charles Lindbergh, Billy Bishop, and other early heroes of the air has survived. And, anyhow, isn't *The Roosevelt and the Antinoe*, through which I suffered in high school, basically journalism in verse? Though it was apparently at one time Pratt's favorite among his poems, it is certainly not (as he admitted) as thrilling as Homer. A journalistic or fictional prose account would surely have been more gripping. Better yet, why not make it into a "disaster" film (and while they're at it, someone should reproduce the Halifax explosion of 1917 in filming *Barometer Rising*).

Similarly, I'd rather read Pierre Berton's version or, better still, listen to Gordon Lightfoot's version of *Toward the Last Spike*.

The documentary poem is, of course, an honorable Canadian tradition, and Pratt is its great progenitor. But such poems sometimes sink under the weight of reportage. I am grateful therefore that Pratt could sometimes forget about accuracy to develop such fantasies as "The Witches' Brew" and "The Great Feud." And it is interesting that the most powerfully imaginative and *resonant* of all his poems — "The Truant" — is also the most fantastic.

What of the man, as revealed here? Well, he was cagey, I suspect. There was someone else behind the camouflage of those anecdotes and sayings. Here he seems determinedly optimistic, folksy, jolly. His tone and style are Victorian and idealistic. He admits to a youthful, naive faith in technology. He stresses the "lighter" side of Newfoundland life even though he mentions the frequency of death and disaster at sea. Perhaps he felt there was enough darkness in the world and in himself that he need not dwell on it in his public utterance (outside the poetry, that is, where a deeper and more ambivalent self may be detected underneath the humanistic and not-very-convincing Christianity).

Pratt was not, I think, much of a poetic theorist, but he was possessed of immense good sense about writing. Both his good sense and his good will shine through this useful book.

1984

2

Last winter I reviewed for *Books in Canada* Susan Gingell's *E.J. Pratt on His Life and Poetry*. In my review I made at least one slightly misleading remark. I said that Pratt "learned early that his poetry had to be made out of the concrete and the material." It is the word "early" that is here misleading; in fact, Pratt was a slow learner who wrote syrupy romantic slush for years before he began to find his own very distinctive voice. But I was more acute, it seems, when I suggested that his well-publicized "personality" was probably a mask. I wrote:

What of the man, as revealed here? Well, he was cagey, I
suspect. There was someone else behind the camouflage of
those anecdotes and sayings. Here he seems determinedly
optimistic, folksy, jolly. . . . [But in the poetry] a deeper and
more ambivalent self may be detected underneath the
humanistic and not-very-convincing Christianity.

This perhaps not very remarkable insight is now fully confirmed by David G. Pitt in his account of Pratt's early life, *The
Truant Years*. Here we meet a boy considered "sickly," a delicate
dreamer who idolized tough and heroic characters but was not
allowed for most of his youth to exert himself very much or to participate fully in Newfoundland life. As a traveling Methodist
preacher's son, expected to behave himself at all times, he was an
outsider to the rough-and-tumble outport life. Pitt writes:

What he had to do . . . was to find a role, a persona or
mask, or several masks, which while shielding and hiding
the sensitive, insecure and vulnerable core of his nature
might also enable him to be, on the visible stage, an actor
whom he himself could admire and who might win the
admiration and approval of others.

Like many another poet (for example, Whitman, or Yeats, or Irving
Layton) he had to create himself as a public character. Though it
took many years, he grew into such a role in mid-life and was not
above making wholly fictional contributions to his own legend.

Pratt became the leading Canadian poet of his time. But it took
him many years of equivocation before he could evade finally and
completely his reluctant promise to his parents that he would give
his life to the Methodist ministry: for years of preaching in pulpits
here and there he had to pretend to a religious zeal he did not feel
in order to please them, as well as to make a meager living. He
managed to remain a kind of professional student through two
PhDs while allowing his mother to believe he would eventually
settle into the ministry.

Privately, Pratt gave himself — even before he wrote poems
about it — to the emotional and intellectual task of salvaging
some humanistic core of values from a bankrupt dogmatic

Christianity and then reconciling this core with the theory of evolution and other scientific developments of the time. For he had since childhood also been obsessed with science and technology.

He was forty before he "found his destiny." Pratt the poet then wanted to counter the all-too-evident terror and violence of existence with a moral vision. But his feelings about the brute force of nature are ambivalent, as many critics have noted. Pitt is quite successful, I think, in accounting for this as he examines Pratt's insecure youth:

> A need to compensate — mostly, I believe, for legacies, real
> or imaginary, of his childhood . . . in various ways
> determined much of his behaviour all his life, in his poetry as
> well as out of it. In his poetry, his fondness for hyperbole,
> verbal and other kinds of heroics, his often obsessive
> preoccupation with brute strength, power, and sheer
> magnitude, and what some critics have called his "juvenile
> delight in violence," are more obvious examples of its
> manifestation.

Pratt wanted, in life and art, to savour his violence and some version of Christian idealism too. He presents the perhaps not uncommon paradox of a genial and just man who nevertheless loves to watch boxing matches and to contemplate with pleasant excitement large disasters. A truly gentle man, his only immediate and personal outlet for aggression seems to have been the golf course; golf obsessed him as much as science, and consumed far more of his time than did poetry.

Pratt laid to rest the painful ghosts of his youth, Pitt says, by making jokes about them. He also told tales that revised his history. After his mother's death, for instance, he told a friend who was writing about him that he had visited her in Newfoundland "every summer until the last," though he had, in fact, been only once in almost twenty years. He would, Pitt says, rewrite the record as he wished it had been. About what touched him most deeply, however, such as the death of his first college sweetheart, he apparently could not write or speak at all. A man of deep and sometimes repressed feelings, he could not be a love poet.

Pitt is very shrewd, I think, in his examination and interpretation of the known facts of Pratt's life. He has probably come as close as one can, given the impossibility of total knowledge of another human being (or of oneself, for that matter), in restoring to us the man hidden behind the partly self-created legend. But though he knew Pratt, and I did not, I wonder if he is not at times a little indulgent. Though I can readily believe that Pratt was a good human being, he was obviously not without faults. His financial follies were surely rather hard on his long-suffering and apparently uncomplaining wife. In his gullibility he once allowed a fancy swindler to carry off not only his own savings but those of his mother-in-law and a number of friends (one of whom committed suicide) whom he had urged to this course of action. They should, of course, have known better. Pratt was notorious for embracing hare-brained get-rich-quick schemes.

His long equivocation about the ministry and his politic refusal to take a stand in the literary wars of modernism might also be seen in a rather less generous light than that cast by Pitt, who seems to feel that his subject was completely without "guile." Yet he reveals of Pratt that "from the early 1930s to the 1950s there were few anthologies of poetry published in Canada which he did not help to make, usually without credit." While allowing that Pratt probably improved these anthologies, and probably acted from mainly generous motives (he was apparently not paid), I can't help but remark as well that this ubiquitous hidden editorship suggests the spectre of an unacknowledged literary dictator. Fortunately, this sort of thing could not happen in today's immensely more pluralistic literary community, where even Margaret Atwood is only one of many centers of authority.

But these quibbles are speculative and subtract nothing from the author's considerable achievement in bringing "Ned" Pratt the man to life again. Pitt usefully explores and illuminates that "dual or split sensibility" which eventually drove Pratt to make a poetry that attempted to reconcile the so-called two cultures of humanism and science. This was Pratt's literary mission, his genuine ministry. As he matured in it, he also constructed for himself a "convivial" persona with which to engage the world, behind which, however (as his wife attested), there lurked always the "other self," a deeply sensitive and vulnerable nature which his youth had conditioned him to attempt to conceal.

1985

3

The Master Years is the second volume of D.G. Pitt's rather masterful biography of E.J. Pratt. While I'm afraid I don't find it quite so absorbing as the first, which documented the making of a highly individual poet, it is still quite often entertaining as an exhaustive chronicle of the years of Pratt's great successes and his lionization by the Canadian establishment of his day. Mackenzie King, Louis St. Laurent, and Lester Pearson were only three of his most distinguished admirers. Unlike most poets, he became a public figure, a kind of unofficial poet laureate. He was showered with honors, degrees, and awards before his death in 1964.

This "national" poet had a good and enjoyable mid-life, in spite of meager finances that were not enhanced either by his own habit of throwing lavish banquets for his cronies or by his daughter's recurrent debilitating and expensive illnesses. A close friend, Arthur Phelps, described Claire Pratt's long illness as "the great tragedy of Ned's life," a dark anxiety that cast a shadow on his generally quite sunny existence. But he nevertheless enjoyed a close and loving relationship with his daughter, and encouraged her in the difficult task of making a life of her own. And though he had to work hard the year around as a teacher to support his family — since increasing fame as an author never translated into what he called "hard cash" — he greatly enjoyed teaching, especially at the Queen's University summer school, partly because his favorite golf course was handy.

Pratt was almost unfailingly gregarious and genial, one reason for his personal popularity with just about everyone who met him, but he was also a skilled literary politician with the politician's occupational deviousness. He pretended to be younger than he was (a minor vanity), told journalists and even friends partly or wholly fictional stories about himself (thus enhancing his "legend"), and

concealed from a possibly unsympathetic public the fact that he
and his work had been greatly affected by the séances in which he
participated in 1928. (It's not known, incidentally, whether Pratt
and Mackenzie King ever discussed this common interest, though
they had dinner together and had at least one medium in common.)
He did later mention these sessions to critic John Sutherland but
would not allow him to raise the subject in his book. He also pretended to have no prior knowledge of this book when it appeared in
1956, though he had read the manuscript and commented on it, privately thinking some of it "fantastic nonsense" but feeling too
flattered and pleased at being taken that seriously to tell the
author as much.

   The séances mentioned above suggest a rather more mystical
Pratt than the one who could speak in public of "beating" the raw
data of history into poetic form in such works as *The Titanic* and
The Roosevelt and the Antinoe. But the typical Canadian documentary artist, who does detailed and painstaking historical research,
can certainly be a visionary as well: witness Pratt's *Brébeuf and His
Brethren* or Rudy Wiebe's *The Temptations of Big Bear*.

   Pratt was discreetly left-wing in politics; he believed in greater
friendship with the Soviet Union but removed the evidence from
his guest book that he had ever entertained Soviet visitors after
the Gouzenko Affair helped to usher in the Cold War. He got on
well, after all, with big capitalists on the golf course while disapproving of their class. He was "pulled both ways at once" political-
ly, it seems, as well as aesthetically.

   Pratt's peculiar position in the history of Canadian literature is
that of transitional poet: in some respects resolutely Victorian and
in some respects (in such classic short poems as "Silences" and
"Come Away, Death") a modern. He hobnobbed with the old
romantics Charles G.D. ("Charley") Roberts and Bliss Carman, but
also got on well with Earle Birney, a close younger friend, and with
Frank Scott, A.J.M. Smith, and A.M. Klein when he chanced to
meet with them. But he resented the modernism and iconoclasm
of the Montreal group (those "bastards," "Montreal egomaniacs,"
and "callow quasi-literates") more and more as he got older —
even though he had a public, not to mention a loyal publisher,
when they did not. But he was not consistent; he disliked the idea

of Irving Layton till he met him, then pronounced him a good fellow, and in ailing old age turned up at the launching of Layton's *Red Carpet for the Sun* to greet the younger poet with the mischievous question: "How are your gonads?"

According to Pitt, the festive E.J. Pratt saw himself "as King Arthur, Prospero, Bacchus, and a benevolent God of creation" when he was entertaining his friends. In the early 1940s he threw a dinner for the visiting A.J.M. Smith at which the guests included Earle Birney, poet Robert Finch, and the young Robertson Davies. Other Toronto friends were Morley Callaghan and the young Northrop Frye. Pratt seems to have been happiest when fraternizing with these and others of "the boys."

Perhaps it's best to conclude, though, with the Kingston connection. Pratt taught ten summers at Queen's, which he called his "second intellectual home." Aside from the Cataraqui golf course, he liked Kingston for its "delightful summer climate," the frolicsome summer friends he made here, and because — though how can he say such a thing? — "Nothing ever changes in Kingston."

1988

4 F.R. Scott's Seminal Influence

1

Pierre Trudeau has said, not entirely in jest, that Frank Scott "taught me everything I know." Scott (born in 1899) is one of the most remarkable Canadians of this century: lawyer, constitutional expert, important member of the CCF and then the NDP, and also (in his spare time) one of that small band of poets who brought literary "modernism" to Canada. His *Collected Poems* won the Governor-General's Award for 1981. He had, astonishingly, never won it before.

But then, F.R. Scott's other achievements as lawyer, social democrat, liberal internationalist, and civil libertarian have always rather overshadowed his poetry. The son of Archdeacon Frederick George Scott, a well-known minor poet of the 1890s, he attended Bishop's, Oxford (as a Rhodes scholar), and McGill early in the century. From 1928 he was a professor of constitutional law at McGill; he retired in 1965 as Dean of the Faculty. He was a founder of the highly influential League for Social Reconstruction in 1932. He later helped to draft the Regina Manifesto of 1933, and served as CCF National Chairman from 1942 to 1950. In 1952 he was Resident Representative in Burma for the United Nations Technical Assistance Program. During the 1950s he fought and won several important civil liberties cases in Duplessis' repressive Quebec; he broke the notorious "padlock law" and later defended *Lady Chatterley's Lover* (or "went to bat for the Lady Chatte," as he puts it in a poem) against charges of obscenity. In the 1960s he was a member of the Royal Commission on Bilingualism and Biculturalism. In the late 1970s his collected *Essays on the Constitution* won the Governor-General's Award for Non-fiction. As a successful radical who has lived into old age, Frank Scott has, ironically, long been lionized as a member of the Canadian establishment; it is interesting that he should be constitutional mentor to a man who gave us not only the new Charter of Rights but also the War Measures Act. But such are the contradictions of federalism and the Quiet Revolution in Quebec.

What of the poetry then? Can a public man of Scott's extraordinary distinction really be an important poet as well? We now have all the evidence in one place: 295 pages of poems and 58 pages of translations (almost all from French, almost all of these from Quebec poets past and present), arranged under eleven headings.

Certainly there is more of Scott's poetry than I had realized. There are very early poems, landscape poems, social satires, war poems, travel poems, love poems, elegies, metaphysical observations, light verses, "found" poems, and the translations, which make a fitting and impressive conclusion to the volume. Scott's eloquent versions of their work have made the very important Quebec poets St.-Denys-Garneau and Anne Hébert more accessible to English readers. This is highly valuable, for I find more insight into the Québécois psyche past and present in the work of these two poets than in a hundred histories and Royal Commission reports.

The quality of Scott's own work ranges from much quite ephemeral verse to accomplished and graceful poems that have so far stood the test of time, as well as a number of pieces that have long and rightly been recognized as Canadian classics. Best known of these, of course, are the funny ones: "W.L.M.K.," "The Canadian Authors Meet," "Bonne Entente," and a few others. Perhaps "W.L.M.K.," which presents Mackenzie King as the embodiment of our national spirit (or lack of it), is the most quotable:

> How shall we speak of Canada,
> Mackenzie King dead?
> . . . . .

He skilfully avoided what was wrong
Without saying what was right,
And never let his on the one hand
Know what his on the other hand was doing.
      . . . . .

He seemed to be in the centre
Because we had no centre,
No vision
To pierce the smoke-screen of his politics.

Truly he will be remembered
Wherever men honour ingenuity,
Ambiguity, inactivity, and political longevity.

Let us raise up a temple
To the cult of mediocrity,
Do nothing by halves
Which can be done by quarters.

It can be argued that there was much more to King than this indicates, but the poem is nevertheless very funny and very telling; and it is implicit in it that the public King was only what we allowed him to be.

Frank Scott and Dorothy Livesay were the important poets of social protest in the 1930s. In his social poems Scott is very direct, if sometimes ironic or sarcastic:

Here is a marvelous new serum:
Six injections and your pneumonia is cured.
But at present a drug firm holds the monopoly
So you must pay $14 a shot — or die.

This is from a sequence called "Social Notes, 1932." It was written long before medicare (which is currently having its difficulties with doctors who think they aren't rich enough) and all the other social programs that Scott and others of the Canadian left gradually persuaded Mackenzie King and his successors to adopt. Perhaps poetry does sometimes help to make things happen.

More important still, in my opinion, and more impressive as poetry are those works in which Scott's social vision and his vision of the land are fused. "Lakeshore," "Trans Canada," and "Laurentian Shield" are probably the best of these. In such poems Scott suggests a larger vision of Canada, one that attempts to define humanity's place in a vast and inhuman but beautiful universe of space-time in flux; in this he resembles Archibald Lampman, Duncan Campbell Scott, and E.J. Pratt before him, his friend and fellow poet of Montreal A.M. Klein, and such poets as Earle Birney, Irving Layton, and Al Purdy after him. (Purdy, for good reason, dedicated his *North of Summer* poems "to Frank Scott.") Thus he is firmly placed in the mainstream of Canadian poets.

All of these poets have been acutely aware of the reaches of time and space that impinge upon us in our largely empty northern land. "All time is present time," Scott writes. "I feel huge mastodons / Press my ape-fingers on this typewriter / Old novae give bright meaning to my words" ("Time As Now"). And of Canada:

Hidden in wonder and snow, or sudden with summer,
This land stares at the sun in a huge silence
Endlessly repeating something we cannot hear.
Inarticulate, arctic,
Not written on by history, empty as paper,
It leans away from the world with songs in its lakes
Older than love, and lost in the miles.
("Laurentian Shield")

In this excellent poem Scott wittily comments on the land's exploitation for profit. But he also concludes:

. . . a deeper note is sounding, heard in the mines,
The scattered camps and the mills, a language of life
And what will be written in the full culture of occupation
Will come, presently, tomorrow,
From millions whose hands can turn this rock into children.

1982

2

Sandra Djwa's biography of F.R. Scott, *The Politics of the Imagination*, tells the story of Scott the public man very well. She is somewhat reticent, however, about the private man — at least after his youth as a younger son in a remarkable Montreal family. His father, Canon F.G. Scott, was an ardent, energetic, and popular muscular-Christian and British imperialist who, as a courageous and comforting middle-aged chaplain, threw himself into the thick of carnage in the First World War without ever losing his naive faith in empire and glory. As a youth Frank Scott shared these attitudes, but later channeled his own idealism into Canadian nationalism, pacifism, social reform, and a modernist poetics. But his father, a minor Victorian poet, considered himself some kind of socialist too, so there was continuity as well as rebellion in the directions in art and life taken by the son. Still, his radicalism offended plutocratic old English Montreal for many years, and estranged him from his conservative older brother, William.

Young, earnest, priggish Frank Scott, a colonial anglophile at Oxford, expressed distaste for jazz and flappers. But in later years he became a Canadian nationalist as well as a bon vivant who liked night clubs and was fond of ladies. Just how his personal transformation came about is not made altogether clear. But a gradual process of liberation is apparent. Dwja is well qualified as a literary historian of Canadian cultural development in the 1920s and 1930s to set the stage for this. The poetry and fiction of D.H. Lawrence combined with Scott's friend A.J.M. Smith to influence his literary development, while CCF leader J.S. Woodsworth came to replace his father as a courageous moral example in public life.

Scott, who died in 1985, seems to have been a man of control and intellect but also of strong, somewhat repressed feelings. This can be a limitation (or sometimes, more happily, a fruitful tension) in his verse. Sandra Dwja indicates discreetly the nature of important dramas in Scott's personal life in the 1940s and again in the 1950s without giving names or details. It's hard to see what else she could have done, while the major players are still alive, but this understandable and even commendable reticence means that a more complete "life" of Scott, one that relates such personal material to his poems, has yet to be written. Even Scott's wife of almost sixty years, Marian Dale, a distinguished artist in her own right, is somewhat anonymous here, though her career and some of her political views are mentioned.

But this is still a most valuable book precisely because it demonstrates so well the public Scott's seminal influence in several areas of Canada's cultural life. He taught a number of distinguished lawyers, politicians, and civil servants (including Robert Bourassa and Michael Pitfield, who, on behalf of Trudeau, sought his advice by phone during the F.L.Q. crisis). He translated important Québécois poets. He also befriended and helped many of the best anglophone poets now growing ever more senior since his death: P.K. Page, Irving Layton, Leonard Cohen, Louis Dudek, D.G. Jones, Phyllis Webb, and Al Purdy.

I would not rate Scott quite so high on the scale of poetic achievement as Sandra Djwa does. But I like her characterization of his best poems, so I'll give her the last word: "His best work is a rare combination of intelligence and deep feeling; curiously, however, this feeling is generated through a surface reticence that creates a tension between expressed and unexpressed emotions. In the finer poems these qualities unite, giving the poems resonance."

1987

5 Irving Layton's Heroics

1

I have always liked very much without knowing extremely well Irving Layton's third wife, Aviva. I think I met her first in Montreal in April 1970. I was there with Seymour Mayne, whose newest poems I was publishing at Quarry Press (then a tiny offshoot of *Quarry Magazine*). I know I stayed overnight at the Laytons' house in order to drive back to Kingston with Irving. He was commuting between Montreal and Toronto regularly at that time. I remember we talked about Canadian poetry, and he remarked that maybe if you put all the Canadian poets together you might have a great poet — a remark considerably more modest than many quoted by Elspeth Cameron in her biography, *Irving Layton: A Portrait*.

To return to Aviva: she endeared herself to me later that spring at a tribute to poet Milton Acorn at Grossman's Tavern in Toronto by calling me "Leonard" without noticing this slip. I was mildly flattered (though I bear no physical resemblance whatever to the Leonard I thought she had in mind). On a later occasion in the 1970s — I think at their house in Toronto where I saw them a few times, once invited for dinner, and I think twice for drinks — I spoke of Ingmar Bergman's *Scenes from a Marriage*, and she said (words to this effect): "Oh, Irving and I have been through all that — several times." The biography fully bears this out.

Aviva is a charming and funny lady. (I've also met two of Layton's other important ladies, Musia Schwartz and fourth wife Harriet, but only briefly.) And I've always liked Irving too, without ever being one of his intimates or (heaven help them) disciples. He can be extremely pleasant and unpretentious in private. He has also been generous to younger writers. I've met him from time to time since readings he did at Queen's University in the early 1960s when his career as a poet was finally taking off after years of struggle. I last saw him at Toronto's Harbourfront with his newest companion Anna a couple of years ago.

I mention this long but infrequent personal acquaintance partly to get it out of the way, and partly because it makes me wonder if Elspeth Cameron hasn't over-emphasized Layton's obvious theatricality, his flamboyant and often bombastic persona at the expense of his other qualities.

But, of course, the publicity-loving public persona persists: Layton is presently circulating to literary journalists letters to Elspeth Cameron in which he informs her (and the world) that she is an ambitious mediocrity, and worse. He adds in one dispatch: "It would have profited me more had I hung a tape recorder from a cow's neck and tickled her to elicit an appreciative moo from her." As the biography amply demonstrates, such denunciatory (and often amusing) letters to reviewers or former friends such as Louis Dudek are not the late aberrations of an angry senior citizen. (Earle Birney, for instance, is denounced in 1951 as "a lanky hayseed from the provinces" and an "uncoiled tapeworm of asininity" for his review of an early Layton volume.) Cameron was presumably well aware of the hazards of writing the life of someone so volatile who is still very much alive.

Layton is also circulating a list of factual errors. Most of these strike me as rather minor. But his insistence that he was never unfaithful to his marriage vows involves a more serious disagreement. Cameron indicates that Layton's version of distant events often differs from those of his wives. This is perfectly normal, given the fallibility and selectivity of memory. The fictionalizing tendency of memory is probably the biographer's (and historian's) biggest problem.

Layton also accuses Cameron of misreading and distorting his poems. Here I think he is sometimes right. But this doesn't alter the fact that the book presents an absorbing human story very well told.

Layton is by any standard a remarkable human being. Born to poverty and all kinds of deprivation, he was apparently from the beginning cheerful, combative, attention-loving, and (like his remarkable mother) "indomitable." Eventually he made himself into a public figure as well as one of the best poets writing in English. Ignored by his father, he was his mother's favorite. Cameron leans heavily, perhaps too heavily, on this original situation. But as one of the oldest sons in a large family, I think I have some insight into the characteristic behavior of a youngest, most indulged one. Such men usually take it for granted that others, especially women, will always want to look after them and do things for them. They make demands. When they don't get their own way (though, if at all lucky, they more frequently do), they may explode. Rightly or wrongly, Cameron skilfully presents this kind of psychological profile. Layton apparently feels it is fiction.

For the record here are a few salient details of Irving Layton's life. He was born Israel Lazarovitch in Romania in 1912 and came to Montreal with his parents the following year. Educated at McGill University, he earned a Master of Arts degree in political science and economics in 1946. He had a number of part-time teaching jobs while publishing numerous poems; from 1969 to 1978 he was a professor of English at York University in Toronto. He received the Governor General's Award for 1959 for *A Red Carpet for the Sun* and has since been nominated for a Nobel Prize. Since 1945 he has written or edited some fifty volumes of verse.

I have sometimes speculated to myself that Layton, like such other poets as Yeats or E.J. Pratt, largely made himself up as he matured, but the recollections of his family suggest that he was always pretty much the same lively and highly emotional person he is now. His charm and genuine concern for others was always a counterweight to his egocentricity and elusiveness. Cameron stresses this last quality as she depicts a man "zig-zagging" among disparate roles and worlds. But surely most, perhaps all, creative people are thus "elusive" to a degree. They can't be "possessed" (except by art), tied, or pinned down.

Cameron commits what seem to me to be errors, or at least

errors of emphasis — some fairly trivial. Surely she is wrong about the location of D.G. Jones's cottage (I've been there); it was near Bancroft, not in Kingston at Royal Military College. Her first mention of Al Purdy suggests, misleadingly, that he originated in Vancouver. (Surely she knows more about the history of Canadian poetry than that.) The aspiring poet (now, I believe, a politician) mentioned on p. 237 is surely John Paul *Harney*, not Harvey. Jane Powell, whom Aviva felt she resembled, was primarily a singer, not a dancer, or is it my memory of the 1950s that is at fault? R.G. Everson, who is presented here as a bourgeois poetic groupie, is in fact a fine poet in his own right. Though the late Desmond Pacey complained that he was having trouble finding any good poets under thirty for a 1965 Canadian number of the American *Literary Review* he included several: Margaret Atwood, Frank Davey, John Newlove, and myself. And finally, something Cameron could not know is that *Time* magazine's account of a party here in Kingston in 1964 for Layton, Birney, Leonard Cohen, and Phyllis Gotlieb was at least partly fabricated and incomplete (that is, somewhat censored) though essentially accurate.

Desmond Pacey was a good friend to Irving Layton, offering him immensely sensible advice and criticism by mail. He warned Layton about rhetoric becoming a bad habit. Perhaps he didn't realize that Layton had always been a rhetorician (like his mother with her rhyming curses) both before and after he was a poet. Leonard Cohen also comes across as a loyal friend, but of a more or less uncritical kind; his account of an LSD trip, during which Irving communed first with the great writers of history and then with his dead mother, is rather delightful.

Needless to say, the accounts of Irving's marriages are extremely interesting, whatever inaccuracies they may contain. Cameron concludes her portrait with a scene in which Layton, curled up like a child, lies sleeping while Betty and Aviva, wives two and three, and his present companion Anna fondly observe him.

Irving once remarked to me that he liked being related, sort of, to Tommy Douglas, one-time father-in-law of his second wife's much younger half-brother, actor Donald Sutherland (if you can follow all that). "You mean, twice removed by divorce," I quipped, thus earning a laugh from Irving and Aviva. But apparently Irving and Betty Sutherland were not legally divorced until the late 1970s,

after which he legally married Harriet Bernstein. Aviva here testi-
fies to the insecurity and anxiety her unmarried state caused her.

Obviously, I found the book absorbing. Whether it is entirely
fair to Irving Layton (indeed, whether *any* biography can present its
subject as God might see him) is a question I won't try to answer.
Instead, I'll give the last word to poet Jay Macpherson: " . . . under
all the rubbish there's that splendid poet. . . . I wouldn't wish to see
an exemplary husband-father-neighbour replace the author of 'A
Tall Man Executes a Jig.'"

1985

2

Waiting for the Messiah is Irving Layton's own version of his early
life. In it he recounts the "myth" that his poet's imagination has
made of his childhood. Born circumcised, he was apparently the
wonder of his Roumanian village; rabbis journeyed, according to his
mother, from as far as Poland and Russia to view the "miraculously
fore-shortened member" of the child who might be their Messiah.
The author enlists, on the first page of this memoir, Moses,
Buddha, and Alexander as infants similarly marked for greatness. "I
was," he writes, "born into a world of fable, a world of stories
charged with significant meanings, the world of the Jews." Family
stories caused him to "feel there was something mysterious and
awesome about my life."

Well. Such a feeling can make for unshakable determination and
a driving rage to prevail. Small wonder, then, that Israel Lazarovitch,
reborn as Irving Layton, poet, should develop in adult life the myth
of the poet as messianic conquering culture-hero or saviour who
awakens his slumbering philistine and bourgeois Canadian country-
men to the glories and horrors of life beyond the commonplace. I am
inclined to think that all potential artists feel special and somehow
separated from others in childhood, but Layton had the peculiar
authority of his folkloric old-war origins to reinforce this feeling.

He grew up in a rough and tumble Montreal world of poverty
and anti-semitism, but his imagination could feed on the other
world of "saviours and messiahs." His pragmatic, tough mother

and his ineffectual, otherworldly father came to epitomize for him the two sides of his nature.

As a schoolboy Issy Lazarovitch was an *enfant terrible* or class clown who once put a dead rat in a teacher's drawer. Like many unusually imaginative individuals, he was bored with school much of the time, yet eventually made his way in the world by acquiring some higher education and becoming a teacher himself. The schoolboy's war with his teachers (immortalized in Mordecai Richler's account of Baron Byng High School in *The Apprenticeship of Duddy Kravitz*) also taught him lessons that would be useful to the controversialist and polemicist he was already becoming: "Self-righteousness, cunning, and the intuitive sense of knowing when to press your advantage are an unbeatable combination." He adds: "That's how political agitators are made."

Layton's account of his difficult but stimulating childhood is quite moving at times — almost Dickensian. It tends to confirm my growing conviction that a certain amount of difficulty and unhappiness (but not too much) plus an innate curiosity and enthusiasm for living help to produce the most successful artists. Layton's childhood was, it seems, rather harsher and more deprived than the one Al Purdy, a poet of comparable stature, writes of in his recent memoir *Morning and It's Summer*, but it is interesting to note that both poets lost their fathers very early on.

Young Layton aspired to be a political agitator. He flirted ambivalently with socialism and had a communist girlfriend whose mother, a veteran of the revolution, took her back to Russia. Only gradually did he realize that he was destined to be a different kind of messiah. The latter part of the book carries him beyond his political activities to deal with his first two wives and his impressions of fellow poets A.M. Klein, Louis Dudek, F.R. Scott, A.J.M. Smith, John Sutherland, P.K. Page, and Patrick Anderson. These glimpses of literary Montreal when it was still the fountainhead of modernist Canadian poetry are very interesting, even if Layton seems (as always) anxious to protest his own superiority as a poet. It is amusing to picture the graciously patrician P.K. Page, young and beautiful, telling brash young Irving that he should study Buddhism to temper the anger that has always been one of his main sources of energy and power.

Layton's account of his first marriage inadvertently reminds one of his objections to Elspeth Cameron's recent biography. He says he married Faye Lynch, a kind but hugely obese woman who had to shave her cheeks daily, out of a kind of morbid pity; Cameron suggests, citing a remark from one of Layton's brothers, that he did it because, in those years of depression, Faye had some money. Certainly it was a very strange match for the energetic and explosive (though, by his own account, sexually inexperienced) young man to make. His union with the beautiful, unconventional, and talented painter Betty Sutherland is much easier to understand.

This is an attractive and very readable account of the youth of a remarkable poet — not, perhaps, the messiah, and certainly no saint. Even in deprived and confusing circumstances, Layton makes us feel there is something wonderful about being young. And he even offers a wise corrective to the messianic hubris his family may have encouraged: "What if the Messiah is life itself, whose sparkling and dithyrambic inflections ask us not to wait but to see and enjoy here and now?"

1985

6 Al Purdy's Stature

Dennis Lee's "Afterword" to Al Purdy's *Collected Poems* attempts to define this man's place among the important poets of the century. Despite some occasional rhetorical overkill, Lee does this very well in an exceptionally fine piece of critical writing. He notes how Purdy's poems range widely and easily in space and time, embodying in their very flow "the intuition that all time and space are simultaneous." Purdy's poetry is "polyphonic" in its great flexibility of voice and tone. In the 1960s and after he has made a Canadian breakthrough into "native speaking" analogous to those of other parts of the world that were formerly hinterland to the old imperial culture centers. For as these centers have declined eloquent new idioms have sprung up in the former colonies.

Thus Purdy is, as Lee has noted before, our Whitman and, at the same time, a very different poet from Whitman. He is "among the finest of living poets, and one of the substantial poets in English of the century." Unfortunately, only a few outside the Canadian literary community are yet aware of this; but our location next to the glare of the United States virtually ensures that any middling American poet can generate far more publicity than a Canadian of comparable or superior gifts. But Lee has no doubts about Purdy's ultimate stature, and neither do I. I have thought for some years that he is (along with Margaret Avison, but that's another story) the finest and most important of English-Canadian poets.

I have written about Purdy's work before: in my book on

Canadian poetry, *Harsh and Lovely Land,* and in an article about what I think poetry is and does, included in this book. I suspect I have little to add at this moment about the greatest poems of the 1960s and early 1970s. "Remains of an Indian Village," "Transient," "The Country North of Belleville," "The Horseman of Agawa," "The Runners," "My Grandfather's Country," and others are already classics. What *is* worth noting now is that after a certain amount of repeating himself with somewhat less distinction in the mid- to late-1970s Purdy has emerged anew in the 1980s with a greater refinement and high-definition than ever in his recent collections *The Stone Bird* and *Piling Blood.* These latest poems have an easy authority that transcends the marvelously Canadian insecurity and self-deprecation that were built into the polyphonic flow of the earlier work.

One example that was published in *Queen's Quarterly* is "Menelaus and Helen," a dramatic monologue in which Menelaus demystifies the story of Helen and Troy but at the same time confirms that wonder and magic (and horror) in the ordinary that has long been part of Purdy's stock in trade. Menelaus remarks: "I will not say / that I grew tired of Helen, but those blue eyes / in which you think to see the sea and see / emptiness, discontent, see the receding / tides of love, deep slumber of the gods — / Besides, she nagged me." He is bemused by the boredom and bloodlust that accompany Helen's beauty and by his growing realization that power and kingship are meaningless dreams. It is a fine and subtle meditation on the banality of evil, on unregenerate human nature in ancient and modern times alike. (Whether there is any connection between this poem and Gwendolyn MacEwen's translation of Yannis Ritsos' "Helen," I do not know: they have somewhat similar implications.)

From first to last Purdy is a poet who glimpses an eternal mystery lurking in the ordinary here and now. Perhaps this temperament is at least partly a genetic inheritance from his more conventionally religious and (I would guess) more imaginatively limited mother. As I have written before, and as Dennis Lee says in his own way, Purdy's version of faith seems to be intuitive. Fatherless from the age of two, he has lacked any too-fixed sense of self-definition (despite the alternately rollicking and sardonic persona of the most engaging comic poems and the poetry reader's lectern) and has displayed instead a lion's share of that Keatsean negative capability that allows the poet — Keats had Shakespeare in mind — to *be* (to fade in and out of) what he observes and presents. There is here great and generous empathy both with other human beings and with the environment. The poet *becomes* the social and natural and cosmic landscape, as in A.M. Klein's classic poem "Portrait of the Poet as Landscape." Indeed, Purdy's "Transient" enacts with greater immediacy that swallowing of the world through the senses and its re-creation in language that Klein describes as the poet's function. It is a function that Purdy continues to perform with enormous distinction for Canada and beyond.

1987

7 Leonard Cohen's Sexual Mysticism

1

Death of a Lady's Man is a kind of notebook consisting of prose poems, loosely constructed free verse, ballads, and lyrics; most of it is concerned with the difficulties of the marriage relationship. It is a better book, I think, than Leonard Cohen's previous return to print, *The Energy of Slaves*, but it is also well below the standard set by his most successful prose and lyrics of the past. There is simply too much self-indulgent surrealism, too much of what has the effect of (not very interesting) automatic writing, too much repetition of idea and effect. The book would certainly have benefited from some pruning. I suspect that anyone other than the most confirmed Cohen addict and vicarious participant in the Cohen legend (of whom, however, there are probably still a good many) will enjoy parts of it while finding the whole just a little tiresome. Certainly that has been my experience.

The book begins well enough with "I knelt beside a stream," which announces the theme of "the obscene silence of my career as a lady's man" and seems to promise a story of sorts. But thereafter nothing happens. Instead we get a great many such declarations as "Disguised as a hat I will rip off your eyebrows," along with the occasional very pointed and effective piece such as "This Marriage" or

"How to speak poetry" or the sonnet paradoxically titled "You Have No Form."

The Cohen protagonist looks for God in sexual love, but domesticity cramps his style even though it is necessary to him. A part of him wants to be thin, free, aspiring, lonely: "My face is too fat. This is the mind of marriage." The poet in him is not to be domesticated, but of course we knew that as long ago as *The Favourite Game.* "You cannot breathe," he writes. "Because you cannot uphold your separation. Because your strangerhood is defeated." He told us when he came he was a stranger.

Many of Cohen's earlier songs and poems are goodbye songs for this reason. The speaker glories in leaving love behind, in having only transient loves, in making his emotion and the love-object herself perfect and impersonal by terminating the affair. Life is raw material for art, or for the religious sense of Mystery that the lover attempts to keep alive in this fashion. It is a popular fantasy with wide appeal to men and women, as Bliss Carman also knew: the romantic wanderer, always a stranger everywhere he goes, leaving his magic touch on many lovers. It is, as Michael Ondaatje has observed in his book on Cohen, the lover and not the beloved who is glorified in this myth; small wonder, then, that the lady of this book has several names but no real identity or character.

Well, there's been a certain development in that a "wife" and children have entered the picture, and it is the conflict between poet-seeker and husband — in Greece, Montreal, or California — that provides what focus there is in this very uneven book. The woman is, by turns, inspiration of and obstacle to the man's artistic and religious striving. "I blame those closest to me for ruining my talent," he writes.

Beyond the expression of the Cohen protagonist's problem, which *does* in its rather extreme way speak for us all, *Death of a Lady's Man* conveys remarkably little, other than a now very familiar public personality. This seems strange when one recalls the great wealth of ideas and insights in *Beautiful Losers.* I felt at the time of the publication of *Beautiful Losers* that Leonard Cohen could employ his extraordinary and unique talent most impressively as a novelist. Perhaps he'll do it yet.

Meanwhile, he has earned, with the best of his songs, poems, and prose, some claim to our indulgence. And there are, for Cohen fans, a few pieces here that are as good or nearly as good as the best work of the past. If the poet's mystical and religious yearnings seem a trifle unfocussed, it seems quite likely that he prefers that. Writing of his book he suggests (rightly or wrongly) that there could be no obvious or neat form for his experience: "I had pledged my deepest health to work this out. The working was way beyond this book. I see this now. I am ashamed to ask for your money. Not that you have not paid more for less. You have. You do."

1979

2

A good deal of Leonard Cohen's writing makes one want to characterize him as a sexual mystic. The well-known poem-song "Suzanne," for example, presents a sexual Madonna ("Our Lady of the Harbour") whose wisdom of flesh and spirit reconciled is, implicitly, even more complete in its healing power than that of Jesus the "Sailor." Here Cohen resembles a Jewish D.H. Lawrence; in *The Man Who Died*, one of his last fictions, Lawrence had fused a bodily-resurrected Jesus with Osiris the lover of the goddess Isis, thus eclectically mixing his mythologies as Cohen was also to do. And *Beautiful Losers* seems a more extreme expression of the longing for a reintegration of mind and body.

Cohen's earlier "Sisters of Mercy" were decidedly sexual. But in *Book of Mercy*, the fifty "psalms" that mark the author's fiftieth birthday, we get his religious yearning minus the sexuality. Not that he renounces sexuality; it is simply not central here. And other past concerns such as drugs and madness have similarly fallen away from the seeker's path to God. Perhaps, then, we must begin to take seriously his previous book's announcement of the "death" of Leonard Cohen the "lady's man."

Many of the psalms suggest a renewed search for God that comes out of the failure of earthly love and the emptiness of worldly success:

In the eyes of men he falls, and in his own eyes too. He falls
from his high place, he trips on his achievement. He falls to
you, he falls to know you. It is sad, they say. See his disgrace,
say the ones at his heel. But he falls radiantly toward the
light to which he falls. They cannot see who lifts him as he
falls, or how his falling changes, and he himself bewildered
till his heart cries out to bless the one who holds him in his
falling. And in his fall he hears his heart cry out, his heart
explains why he is falling, why he had to fall, and he gives
over to the fall. Blessed are you, clasp of the falling. He falls
into the sky, he falls into the light, none can hurt him as he
falls. Blessed are you, shield of the falling. Wrapped in his
fall, concealed within his fall, he finds the place, he is
gathered in. While his hair streams back and his clothes tear
in the wind, he is held up, comforted, he enters into the place
of his fall. Blessed are you, embrace of the falling, foundation
of the light, master of the human accident.

This is the whole of No. 8. In the following psalm Cohen writes:
"You are the truth of loneliness, and only your name addresses it.
Strengthen my loneliness that I may be healed in your name, which
is beyond all consolations that are uttered on this earth." In desola-
tion one is turned toward God. God gives "a form to desolation"
(No. 46).

The psalmist expresses a great longing to recover God, grace, the
soul, a spiritual dimension that the modern social world has largely
lost. Here I am reminded of the theme (though not the manner) of
Dennis Lee's most serious poems. I think also of the last section of
A.M. Klein's *The Second Scroll* and of Margaret Avison's devotional poems. Cohen appears to repudiate (at least on some level of
being) his whole previous career — or perhaps it is the public image
and egotism so prominently on display in that career that he repu-
diates — and to embrace emptiness as a way to God.

What the reader makes of this will, of course, depend upon his
or her own religious feelings. Let me say only that these brief
pieces seem to me to be more straightforward and sincere in tone
than a great deal of Cohen's previous baroque or complex, irony-
ridden utterance.

Is this prose poetry, prayer, devotional prose? It is difficult to judge as "literature." But it seems to me that it succeeds as language. The psalms have a simple elegance and unfailing rhythmic grace that are entirely appropriate to the religious sensibility they reveal. This book is probably not Cohen's masterpiece — he is only fifty — but it is a book that one can very much respect.

1984

8 Margaret Atwood's Cool

1

In her book *The Animals in that Country*, Margaret Atwood's by-now-characteristic cool is well kept, making one wonder whether it is not likely to harden soon into a mannerism. Her poems are beautifully made and always intelligent, but a little inhuman. The words seem to fall too perfectly into place: there is already a kind of Atwood formula. But there is excitement too, intellectual excitement, in her best poems, for example, in "Progressive Insanities of a Pioneer":

> If he had known unstructured
> space is a deluge
> and stocked his log house-
> boat with all the animals
>
> even the wolves,
> he might have floated.
>
> But obstinate he

stated, The land is solid
and stamped,

watching his foot sink
down through stone
up to the knee.

. . . in the end
through eyes
made ragged by his
effort, the tension
between subject and object,

the green
vision, the unnamed
whale invaded.

Metaphysics and metaphor: the search for ways in which to define
oneself, to find identity with one's body, one's instincts, one's
country. This *is* genuine pioneering, and in those rare moments
when she approaches the personal Atwood exhibits the capacity
for further development, wider range:

Meanwhile on several
areas of my skin, strange bruises glow
and fade, and I can't remember
what accidents I had, whether I was
badly hurt, how long ago

1969

2

Margaret Atwood's *The Journals Of Susanna Moodie* is her best
book yet. This is so because she appears to have found an effective
objective correlative for her own emotions in the experience of
Susanna Moodie. The book is both personal and objective; it has a

human power to move that the earlier fables of Frankenstein, green giants, and space-men did not have. I wrote a couple of brief passages about Mrs. Moodie myself once, mainly because I felt that *Roughing It in the Bush* expressed the Canadian odyssey or initiation or "growth in awareness though exposure to the wild" or whatever it is we have undergone with an almost archetypal force and clarity, but Margaret Atwood has been able to make more both of the literal and the symbolic possibilities of Mrs. Moodie's life-experience than I could do. Her Moodie becomes one of the ancestral voices, those ghosts who remind us of the beauty and terror of the wilderness within and without that we have yet to be fully possessed by:

> . . . the land shifts with frost
> and those who have become the stone
> voices of the land
> shift also and say
>
> god is not
> the voice in the whirlwind
>
> god is the whirlwind
>
> at the last
> judgement we will all be trees

1970

3

You Are Happy is Margaret Atwood's sixth book of poems, the first since *Power Politics*, which made black comedy out of the destructive games, projections, and illusions of lovers. This is, in a sense, a kind of sequel, in which the protagonist moves forward toward the new country of relationship without false hopes, promises, defences, evasions, mythologies. It is an affirmative book, so I was surprised to see Toronto reviewers going on as usual about Atwood's bleak, relentless, morbid vision as if this were only *Power Politics* revisited. Even the first section, in which the protagonist expresses grief, regret, and remorse (as well as anger) over the failure of a past relationship, is warmer and more sympathetic than any of Atwood's earlier icy (and often accurate) analyses of the wicked ways of men, women, and modern urban societies. My favorites among her earlier books, *Surfacing* and *The Journals of Susanna Moodie*, perhaps foreshadowed the development that is found here.

The book's second section, "Songs of the Transformed," contains marvelously imaginative poems spoken by humans who have been changed into animals. From this perspective "there are no angels/but the angels of hunger"; these poems get down to the basic realities of hunger and death. All life is predatory, and all of us are transformed to corpses in the end. In the third section, "Circe/Mud Poems," the problem of the sexual relationship is re-explored in terms of the story of Circe and Ulysses; again, this is a highly imaginative treatment in which Circe's enchanted island is recognizably a Canadian rural setting. The section concludes with the suggestion that perhaps the lovers are not after all trapped in that unhappy story. In the fourth section, "There is only one of everything," a man and a woman appear to move, at first tentatively and then with joyous confidence, toward the new kind of relationship described above. The cruelty of myth has been left behind, the sacrifice and offering are voluntary, and in this there is freedom. In earlier Atwood collections one felt that even the body was regarded as a prison, but here it is singled out for praise.

The book seems, then, to be a turning point in the poet's development. Technically, too, it is an advance over *Power Politics*. Many individual poems from that book tend to lose their force when removed from the context of the whole sequence; moreover, some of the shock-tactics and surreal effects seem to me inadequate to the psychological processes they are attempting to represent. Here there is more technical variety than in the past, manifesting itself partly in an effective use of the prose poem; one feels that most poems are autonomous and interesting in and for themselves, as is each of the four sections, and yet all contribute to a coherent whole — a human statement, a journey. I think we may be grateful to Margaret Atwood for facing up to the most difficult facts of our existence and for putting the case for joy so minimally and so well.

1975

4

Is mid-Atwood as good as early Atwood? Is Margaret Atwood a better poet in prose than in poetry? These are two (perhaps silly) questions aroused by her second selected poems. The first, published in 1976, has sold some 17,000 copies. The author's enviable popularity and reputation are not likely to decline significantly in the very near future. She is just about as established as a writer can be in her own lifetime.

It is interesting that each of Atwood's recent collections seems to me to be somewhat stronger than its predecessor. I was a little surprised to find that the title-poem of _Two Headed Poems_ still bores me; I had thought that this time I might find whatever I was missing in it. But it still reads like so much verbal doodling, I'm afraid; the basic idea might have sustained a much shorter piece. There are, though, some very much better poems in this volume: "Five Poems for Grandmothers," "Marrying the Hangman" (one of those pieces that inspires my second question above), "A Red Shirt," "You begin." The focus on mothers and daughters (especially her own daughter) adds another dimension to the poet's vision. But much of _Two-Headed Poems_ strikes me as serviceable, run-of-the-mill Atwood.

True Stories is, like the novel _Bodily Harm_, her Amnesty International book. It contains powerful poems about a dismayingly common world-wide human activity that most of us here are fortunate enough to know next to nothing about: torture. There are also some nice poems about leaving the countryside, and a very effective piece honouring the scavenging vulture: this witty poem is almost like D.H. Lawrence or Ted Hughes at their best, but compressed.

Murder in the Dark presents highly successful prose-poems. Passages in Atwood's novels (especially _Surfacing_) have similar qualities of wit, wordplay, quiet but insistent rhythmic force (of the kind that many or even most of the "poems" notoriously lack), and surprising but meaningful juxtapositions of objects, words, and images. She excels in this area between fiction and poetry, partly (I suspect) because hers has always been the kind of mildly surreal imagination that can illuminate the "real" world in a fresh way.

When I first read *Interlunar* I felt that this was Atwood's best collection since *You Are Happy*, which served as the climax of her first selected poems. A sly sense of humor (as in the snake poems) balances a grave contemplation of inevitable aging and mortality. Mid-life ought to stimulate one's most mature work, and here this is impressively demonstrated. "Interlunar" itself is one of the finest brief poems Atwood has written. It makes me think that an artist as successful as she may be in an especially good space to evoke that emptiness which is co-existent with plenitude. "Trust me," she writes. "This darkness / is a place you can enter and be / as safe in as you are anywhere." She mentions "stars / above the leaves, brilliant as steel nails / and countless and without regard." Beyond her legitimate feminist and other political concerns there was, in her best poems, always this deeper note.

There are twenty-one new poems to round things off. "Aging Female Poet Sits on the Balcony" shows that Atwood can be funny about the disadvantages of fame. In other poems she turns once again to prose, or else experiments with much longer lines than she has usually employed in the past. Most of these don't engage me as much as "Interlunar" but they do reveal an admirable desire to strike off in new technical directions. Several poems make me think, perhaps mistakenly, of Marian Engel's last years and her death.

This second selected poems is, I feel, less cohesive somehow than the first, and more various. This is both loss and gain; but then that's what mid-life is all about (as Joni Mitchell might say). Atwood's artistic mid-life has (so far) given us a number of excellent poems as well as her most accomplished novel to date, *The Handmaid's Tale*. She is, one feels, far from written out.

1987

9 John Thompson's Darkness

John Thompson died, if I am not mistaken, on the same day late in 1976 on which Stanley Cooperman died. Born an Englishman, Thompson settled on the east coast of Canada; born an American, Cooperman settled on the west coast. At opposite ends of the continent these two poets died, and there is a crazy (or fearful) symmetry here. Even the methods of death, which might be characterized, respectively, as English and ambiguous, and straightforward and American, contribute to this.

Youthful deaths, suicides, madness: these are rare, if not completely unknown, in the histories of the best Canadian poets. (A.M. Klein had a breakdown; Archibald Lampman, Raymond Knister, Red Lane, and Anne Wilkinson died young; Pat Lowther was murdered and seems to have foreknown it. But the solid Pratts, D.C. or F.R. Scotts, Birneys, Laytons, Livesays, Purdys, etc. are more typical; we don't produce Plaths, Lowells, Berrymans, Sextons, Delmore Schwartzes, etc.) So Thompson's early death, like Pat Lowther's, is a temptation to legend-makers. But it is a mistake, I think, to want to manufacture a Canadian Sylvia Plath. What we have here are two fine and still developing poets whose deaths are therefore (for those who think poetry an important register of the collective human psyche) a great pity. But in reading *Stilt Jack* I do not feel that John Thompson's exploration of his own darkness *had* necessarily to lead to his early death. It could as easily have been a purgative and restorative experience. One can exaggerate the romantic poet "maudit" business, and thereby do the poems themselves a disservice. Still, the darkness in the second book is real, and does therefore make one think at times of such poets as Sylvia Plath or John Berryman or (closer to home) of the finest and most controlled outpourings in Gail Fox's *God's Odd Look*.

In Thompson's first book, *At the Edge of the Chopping There Are No Secrets* (1973), the darkness tends to be between the lines. An imagist precision renders the being and mystery of common things domestic and outdoors. But one has a sense as well that these are rendered so concretely and vividly because they are stays against larger confusion (as Robert Frost might say). I am reminded at times of D.G. Jones, especially when Jones and Thompson have in common an interest in Alex Colville's refrigerated crow. And some of the animal poems make one think of Ted Hughes, though Thompson's tone is much quieter. The importance of Yeats to *Stilt Jack* is foreshadowed only momentarily in a phrase like "crazy salads."

Thompson juxtaposes impressions and images very skilfully. The poems are oblique, minimal, imagist. It is a poetry that is too reticent (I suspect) ever to achieve wide popularity, a poetry beautifully and fastidiously made (again, like that of D.G. Jones). Probably, the ghazal as adopted by Thompson in *Stilt Jack* was conceived as a means of extending and enlarging and enriching this spare idiom, of transcending its evident limitations with new leaps and emotional associations.

In *At the Edge of the Chopping* Thompson writes:

> to be possessed or
> abandoned by a god
> is not in the language . . .

But in *Stilt Jack* he declares:

> I'm in touch with the gods I've invented:
> Lord, save me from them.

A new language, a new acquaintance with one's inner demons has intervened and is in process:

I believe in unspoken words, unseen gods:
where will I prove those?

In the opening of *Stilt Jack* there is immediately a new urgency, reminiscent (deliberately) of Yeats and also (for me) of some of Robert Lowell's finest late sonnets:

Now you have burned your books: you'll go
with nothing but your blind, stupefied heart.

Here at once is a deliberate plunge into that darkness that was held at bay in the earlier book. The speaker's domestic haven, and, it would seem, his intellectual and cultural defences as well, have crumbled and left him in the void which he now explores (again, rather as D.G. Jones, whom I shall hereafter leave out of it, does in his very fine poem "I thought there were limits").

The ghazal and the cold passion of Yeats have assisted Thompson here. In his introductory note, the poet describes the ghazal in these terms:

The ghazal proceeds by couplets which (and here, perhaps, is the great interest in the form for Western writers) have no necessary logical, progressive, narrative, thematic (or whatever) connection. The ghazal is immediately distinguishable from the classical, architectural, rhetorically and logically shaped English sonnet.

The link between couplets (five to a poem) is a matter of tone, nuance: the poem has no palpable intention upon us. It breaks, has to be listened to as a song: its order is clandestine. . . .

The ghazal allows the imagination to move by its own nature: discovering an alien design, illogical and without sense — a chart of the disorderly, against false reason and the tacking together of poor narratives. It is the poem of

contrasts, dreams, astonishing leaps. The ghazal has been
called "drunken and amatory" and I think it is.

I am sympathetic to the enterprise described here since I myself
once wrote (without, for better or worse, ever having heard of the
Persian ghazal) a longish sequence, "Islands" (published in 1971 in
Magic Water, my second collection), which was similarly concerned
to allow the demon within a greater freedom of movement and association; I considered the form I invented a sort of "freed sonnet."
    Stilt Jack is highly successful as "song." It moves, always con-
tained by the couplet structure (Thompson sometimes goes beyond
the stipulated five couplets), urgently and vividly from image to
image, thought to thought or question, like one of Lowell's more
successful free sonnets of his last period. A kind of cross-section of a
man's consciousness rendered as sound and rhythm is the "alien
design" thereby achieved. Such a poem is excessively self-regarding,
perhaps, but it is, after all, an inner exploration that is Thompson's
concern here.
    The consciousness that is the poem is full of Yeats:

>   Yeats. Yeats. Yeats. Yeats. Yeats. Yeats. Yeats.
>   Why wouldn't the man shut up?

Yeats is Thompson's opposite, since he lived a long life and wrote
a great deal, re-creating himself in the process. Perhaps, as he jok-
ingly suggests here, Thompson wanted to shut Yeats up, but if so
he finds himself performing this exorcism through a poetic process
in which Yeats provides his main terms of reference (and even his
title, which suggests the rhetorical ambitions of the poet who
wants to walk on stilts, magnify himself). The opening lines, quoted already, remind the reader immediately of

>   I must lie down where all the ladders start,
>   In the foul rag-and-bone shop of the heart.

The Yeatsean "heart" recurs throughout the poem, as does the
Yeatsean fisherman. Thompson's man is both fisherman (like Jay
Macpherson's poet in *The Boatman*) and caught fish, victim of a

predatory universe. "Cast a cold eye" and the "rook delighting heaven" are other Yeatsean properties invoked here. They speak of deprivation, lost love, nakedness, pride — as in "The Fisherman," "The Cold Heaven," "The Circus Animals' Desertion," "Under Ben Bulben."

There are non-Yeatsean allusions as well, usually of lesser importance, and quite likely some that have escaped me. One that *does* rather insist upon itself consists in echoes of Theodore Roethke's line

> I learn by going where I have to go.

This, of course, has at once to do with the freely moving ghazal and with the speaker's exploration of his own possibilities for darkness and light. The two — poem and consciousness — are one process. And the end (or destination) of the process is uncertain, as I suggested before. Either total destruction or renewal is possible:

> when I meet you again I'll be all light,
> all dark, all dark.

> I have only to lift my eyes to see
> the Heights of Abraham.

The poet speaks of a "man dancing into life" but also of death; a woman's love is at times consolation; and yet there is precious little "coming through" (in D.H. Lawrence's sense) in these poems, and much darkness.

There is also some obscurity for the casual reader who has no access to Thompson's range of reference. For instance, Meton, an ancient Greek astronomer, is mentioned (I think) because John Thompson, at the age of 38, had in mind Meton's idea of the 19-year cycles of the moon. At age 38, he was up for possible renewal. (Perhaps this is why the sequence has 38 poems.)

Another allusion in Poem IV I recognized as having to do with "The Marriage of Heaven and Hell," though I couldn't recall exactly what Blake had said. Thompson writes

I'll dream,

lie down on my right side, left side, eat dung:
Isaiah greets me; he wants to talk; we'll feed.

Blake wrote of an interesting dinner conversation with Ezekial and
Isaiah in which the utterances of the Hebrew prophets are interpreted as having to do with "Poetic Genius" as the first principle
of everything and with the true nature of everything that exists as
"infinite":

> I then asked Ezekial why he ate dung, and lay so
> long on his right and left side. He answered, "The
> desire of raising other men into a perception of the
> infinite: this the North American tribes practise, and
> is he honest who resists his genius or conscience only
> for the sake of present ease or gratification?"

Eating dung, swallowing darkness, dreaming could have a positive
purpose then. Blake was surely (with Yeats) the least self-destructive of poets.

In _Stilt Jack_ John Thompson gives us a consciousness on the
knife-edge between darkness, despair, the void, and the heights of
grandeur that he knows are still there in the world. The poet is the
fish caught on that double hook. Where he might have gone from
this acute awareness if he had lived longer is impossible to say. He
would have learned in the continuing, the going on. One possible
area of development for him might have been the public world, more
public human (and extra-human) concerns, since these are scarcely
present (except for a glancing reference early on to terror and disaster
"from America") in _Stilt Jack_. The poem has obvious limitations as
well as impressive strength. And we have lost a valuable poet who
might well have found that he had more to say to us. The diffidence
of the first book had given way to an urgency that could well have
led to a further breakthrough for this unprolific explorer of spaces
and silences who came to live among us so briefly.

1978

10 Michael Ondaatje's Palimpsest

It occurred to me when I set about writing this article that if I was going to find anything more to say about the poems of Michael Ondaatje I would have to try to forget that I had known the poet since the summer of 1965, at which time the early poems that he showed me both puzzled and (intermittently) impressed me. So I have tried to look anew at long-familiar poems, to look at them analytically without (except in one case) reference to my own first experience of them as part of a very immediate exchange of poems, ideas, and personalities with a fellow poet.

The poetry has matured a great deal; my puzzlement has never entirely vanished. In the early poems brilliant and sometimes bizarre imagery often co-existed with what I thought rhythmic and idiomatic awkwardness or oddity. Sometimes the oddity grew on me or seemed eventually to justify itself in terms of a brilliant concept that had escaped me on first reading. Sometimes it did not.

Re-reading the poems, I want to ask certain questions of them, as if I were a high-school textbook. These are perhaps naive (like all the best questions) but they constitute a beginning. Many early poems reveal the poet's aestheticism, and Ondaatje's whole work in poetry and prose reveals an obsession with art and the artist, yet he claims to "hate art" in his poem "War Machine." Why? In "Billboards" he speaks of "trying to live / with a neutrality so great / I'd have nothing to think of." Why does the poet want this "neutrality"? Is this desirable or even possible for a poet? Poems like "Gold and Black" present bizarre images of loss of self and disintegration (as does *The Collected Works of Billy the Kid*), and in "Burning Hills" the poet writes: "Every summer he believed would be his last." (In context this may mean simply the last summer he would write, not imminent death, though the larger significance cannot be dismissed. And in his recent little book *Tin Roof* Ondaatje announces on the first page: "This last year I was sure / I was going to die.") Why does the poet believe this? In "Walking to Bellrock" he himself asks: "Stan, my crazy summer friend, / why are we both going crazy?" Well, if they are, why are they? Does the poem offer any clue? Should the reader be especially concerned about or perhaps even put off by these unsupported suggestions of authorial precariousness or melodrama?

Naive questions perhaps deserve naive answers. But I am not interested in answering them in terms of the particular strains and changes of Ondaatje's personal life (which are not in any case so very different from those of more ordinary mortals). I would like to say, however, that I believe that these questions arise for me because the persona or artist-figure revealed in the poems seems to me to be a rather different person from the sensible, capable, well-balanced, considerate, shrewd, determined, healthily ambitious and competitive, good-humored (he once, at my suggestion, fed to his book-eating pigs a battered old copy of *Animal Farm*), somewhat shy, interestingly tricky and only moderately high-strung, volatile, and moody individual also named Michael Ondaatje whom I know. (Similarly, "Stan" is one of the saner people I have known in or out of Kingston.) All artists are no doubt divided selves (as in Yeats's formulation of "self" and "anti-self"), but the alternative self or life of Ondaatje's work is often a remarkably dramatic and even bizarre one that has had considerable appeal to those readers who have made *Billy the Kid* in particular a long-time best-seller.

Critics Stephen Scobie, Sam Solecki, and others have commented on the author's identification with his historical-fictional personae William Bonney and Buddy Bolden. Both author and reader live vicarious or alternative lives through these figures. I think there is a sense in which the "I" (or sometimes, as in "Burning Hills," a poem more obviously autobiographical than most, the "he") of the shorter poems is also a fictional construction, an anti-self or an exaggeration of certain (sometimes violent) human feelings and possibilities. (The other day I heard filmmaker David Cronenberg explain on the radio that when someone's head literally explodes in his film it is a dramatization of the sensory overload that makes one feel as if one's head "is exploding": Ondaatje, nobody need be surprised to learn, likes horror films just as much as westerns and old swashbucklers like *Scaramouche*.) This is the naive and no doubt obvious answer to my series of naive questions. Ondaatje the artist exaggerates.

The earlier Ondaatje's myth or fiction is often bizarre and, I think, somewhat arbitrary. It is one in which an artist-figure lives on the brink of disaster. He is a killer-spider ("Spider Blues") or a persecuted and deformed monster ("Peter") who hates the world as much as he loves it. Art and the making of beauty, indeed all communication, are for him inseparable from psychic rape or murder or, ultimately, suicide. The artist is both killer and victim in his participation in the processes of an almost wholly predatory universe. Art is for him necessarily exploitation of reality. Thus the poet suspects himself at all times.

I am, as I have indicated before, neither temperamentally nor philosophically inclined to assent wholly to such a world-view. But I can assent in part, I can suspend my disbelief while experiencing the poem, and I can easily admire the brilliance with which the myth is often executed (so to speak).

All of the above remarks have been by way of introduction and to get some general comments and views (or perhaps prejudices) of my own out of the way. What follows is the result of my re-examination of the poems.

It occurs to me in re-reading the poems that the dominant metaphor in Ondaatje's work is "layering" or merging itself. Palimpsest perhaps. His reality involves "billboard posters / blending in the rain" ("Billboards") and "coloured strata of the brain" ("The Gate in his Head"). "The summers were layers of civilization in his memory," we are told in "Burning Hills." Almost all of his earlier poems involve the laying or layering of one landscape, one geographic or temporal or psychic reality, and in the marriage poems even one person, on another. (Even the epigraph added to *The Dainty Monsters* in *There's a Trick With a Knife I'm Learning To Do* projects a human face on the sky, and suggests the necessity of this layering or integration

of fact and dream, world and self, for psychic survival.) This process perhaps begins with the "laying" of Ceylon on Canada. In the early poems
the mythic past, whether personal or historical, is laid on the mundane
Canadian present: new women are projected for the fields between
Kingston and Gananoque ("Early Morning, Kingston to Gananoque").

In "Birds for Janet — the Heron," the first poem in Ondaatje's
selected poems, a suicidal king is superimposed or projected rather
arbitrarily upon a heron (a notion elaborated on later in "Heron
Rex"). In "Dragon," the second poem, a dragon is superimposed on
a beaver (and, behind the poem, on Tom Marshall, since it was I —
I confess — who ran into the badminton net while playing hide-
and-seek at dusk and thus lost my breath — though not, obviously,
forever). In subsequent poems reflection imagery blends the seasons, the worlds of sleeping and waking, of nature and human
dwelling ("The Diverse Causes"); Gary Snyder and his mountains
are superimposed on a hospital scene while the poet is imaginatively spread all over Ontario ("Signature"); Henri Rousseau's dream
landscape is laid on the world of society ladies ("Henri Rousseau
and Friends"); wild nature and man's (not to mention the dog's) savage dreamlife are laid on his domesticity ("Biography," "The
Republic"); passion and instinct are laid on reason and mechanism
(and vice versa), as in *Billy the Kid*; art is frequently laid on life.
Indeed, "layering" may be another way of saying metaphor, and it
may be that, at some level, these poems are "about" the mind's
poetic process itself. This makes the poet's later objections to
"metaphor" and "art" somewhat ironic.

In many poems beauty is laid on violence, or violence on beauty. Layering is sometimes a violent or aggressive transgression of a
boundary, even an internecine war within the poet (as in Dennis
Lee's reading of *Billy the Kid* in *Savage Fields*). "Philoctetes on the
Island" presents the aggressive artist:

> Sun moves broken in the trees
> drops like a paw
> turns sea to red leopard
>
> I trap sharks and drown them
> stuffing gills with sand

cut them with coral till
the blurred grey runs
red designs

A predatory sun laid on sea, and the hunter who kills, making "red designs": here is Ondaatje's world and his subtext of the wounded and wounding artist in a nutshell.

In "Elizabeth" there is historical layering (as there is in *Billy the Kid* and *Coming Through Slaughter*). The presumed twentieth century of "Daddy," "Uncle Jack," and "Mrs. Kelly" is gradually merged with the story of Elizabeth, her sister "Bloody" Mary, Mary's husband Philip of Spain, the unfortunate or perhaps very foolish Tom Seymour, who was thought to have had a sexual dalliance with the young princess and was later executed for political reasons, and her late favorite the Earl of Essex (also, of course, executed — an irony not made explicit in the poem itself). The lively little girl who had an adventure with a snake at the zoo is, by this somewhat suspect poetic trickery, revealed eventually as the aged, already legendary queen. Thus the poem seems to support Gwendolyn MacEwen's assertion that all times and worlds are one. (I expect the young Ondaatje saw Jean Simmons and Stewart Granger in *Young Bess*, as I did.)

In more personal and domestic poems a complex family situation is laid on the poet's "virgin past," the poet's interpretations are laid on his wife's past ("Billboards"), body is laid on brain, numbing it ("Kim, at half an inch"), and wife, "Love, the real," is laid on poet, "the dreamer in his riot cell" ("Gold and Black"). Here fact (flesh) is laid on dream (imagination), but this works the other way around too, as we have seen.

Ondaatje merges with his dog ("The Strange Case"), with his son ("Griffin of the Night"), with Henri Rousseau ("The Vault"), with Darwin ("Charles Darwin pays a visit, December 1971"), with King Kong and Wallace Stevens ("Dates," "King Kong Meets Wallace Stevens"). In "Letters and Other Worlds" he attempts to recover his lost father and his first world as he does at greater length in *Running in the Family*. The search for his father in himself as much as in the world of recoverable fact is analogous to the search *in himself* for Billy or for Buddy. And he assimilates and takes unto himself those he admires and needs in "Taking":

> It is the formal need
> to suck blossoms out of the flesh
> in those we admire
> planting them private in the brain
> and cause fruit in lonely gardens.
>
> To learn to pour the exact arc
> of steel still soft and crazy
> before it hits the page.
> I have stroked the mood and tone
> Of hundred year dead men and women
> Emily Dickinson's large dog, Conrad's beard
> and, for myself,
> removed them from historical traffic.
> Having tasted their brain. Or heard
> the wet sound of a death cough.
> Their idea of the immaculate moment is now.

In "Letters and Other Worlds" Ondaatje credits his father with "complete empathy." The father's life and fate can, of course, be seen as tragic. Nevertheless, "complete empathy" is a rather more positive characterization of the poetic process so often seen in earlier poems as predatory or cannibalistic or suicidal. Perhaps this may even indicate the possibility of a new identification with the real that is now so close that it is no longer an imposition of his private myth on the world or a "suicide into nature" but a reconciliation with the world — a balance that transcends the two poles of destruction and self-destruction. In "Pig Glass," the closing section of the selected poems, something like this may be happening. (And perhaps it was foreshadowed in such earlier poems of relative balance and harmony as "The Diverse Causes" and "We're at the Graveyard.")

In "Pig Glass" there is perhaps a new departure or direction for Ondaatje's poetry. Beyond the self-destructive silence of "White Dwarfs," the powerful last poem of *Rat Jelly*, is a new apprehension of the world simply as it is immediately experienced without obvious "layering" or metaphor. (I am not quite so naive as to say "simply as it is.")

Ondaatje quotes Italo Calvino:

Newly arrived and totally ignorant of the Levantine
languages, Marco Polo could express himself only with
gestures, leaps, cries of wonder and of horror, animal
barkings or hootings, or with objects he took from his
knapsacks — ostrich plumes, pea-shooters, quartzes —
which he arranged in front of him . . .

The poems that follow make such assertions as "All night the truth
happens" ("Country Night") and "There is no metaphor here"
("Walking to Bellrock"). "Country Night" describes the small
events (including small dreams) of the night. "The Agatha Christie
Books by the Window" celebrates avocados and other concrete
objects on Vancouver Island. "Buying the Dog," "Moving Fred's
Outhouse / Geriatrics of Pine," and "Buck Lake Store Auction" are
also predominantly poems of fact. In "Walking to Bellrock," the
most expansive and impressive of these poems, the poet and his
friend Stan seek relief from their unparticularized human craziness
in the immediate physical reality of walking in the river to Bellrock,
so that "all thought / is about the mechanics of this river," which are
then presented vividly and effectively. There is no "history or philosophy or metaphor" here, and instead of myth there is the simple
"plot" to get to Bellrock. (Though, of course, the archetypal critic
might want to argue that all journeys on a river signify the attempt
to get through life itself — here a purely physical existence — more
or less intact.) Other poems describe very directly Ondaatje's
renewed impressions of Ceylon (now Sri Lanka), give Sallie
Chisum's commonsensical late thoughts about Billy the Kid ("He
was a fool"), and arrange the concrete fragments of Ondaatje's experience of fellow poet Chris Dewdney. Indeed, in all of these poems
we get the sort of arrangement of objects indicated in the epigraph
from Calvino.

But the earlier Ondaatje "layering" formula does not altogether
disappear. The erotic poems of Wyatt and Campion are laid on the
present in "Farre Off." There is perhaps archeological layering in
"Pig Glass" itself. In "Sweet like a Crow" all Ceylon is laid on an
eight-year-old girl's raucous voice. In "Late Movies with Skyler" the
Stewart Granger version of *The Prisoner of Zenda* (plus the poet's

past involvement with it) is laid on footloose young Skyler. Even Billy is projected on the night sky in Sallie's mind. Most important-ly (since it brings us in a sense back to the starting gate, and also looks forward to *Running in the Family*), in the beautiful "Light," the last poem of the selected poems, Ceylon and the past (more par-ticularly, the poet's late mother and her family) are laid on a stormy summer night in Canada. The electric storm makes the trees appear to be walking away from the speaker, but in truth they, and by implication the mother and her world, haven't "moved an inch" from him. He is in the process here, as in *Running in the Family*, of recovering that lost world and, in thus healing an old rupture, recov-ering a lost self as well.

For these are poems notably more gentle than most of those in *The Dainty Monsters* or *Rat Jelly* (let alone those in *Billy the Kid*). It seems as if the process of "layering" of past and present, of Ceylon and Canada, of disturbed imagination and Canadian land-scape, of inner and outer, has led, eventually, to a degree of self-realization, self-integration, and reconciliation of these and other polarities that makes possible a new kind of poetry, and perhaps a new anti-mythic "myth" for the poet.

Does the sequence *Tin Roof* (republished in 1984 in *Secular Love*) bear this out? Well, it seems to me to be a transitional poem, sharp in local detail but perhaps a little incoherent in overall struc-ture. We find the poet once again poised on the brink of an unspeci-fied disaster, unspecified, that is, except for the opening remark, already quoted, about dying. He is waiting for "wisdom," a "solu-tion" to his unspecified problem, and perhaps simultaneously for poetic inspiration (like Rilke, whom he eventually addresses), whether it comes as "seraphim or bitch." He watches for "cue cards / blazing in the sky." But he finds no wisdom thus projected or "layered" on the world, only the specifics of the place, a cabin on the Pacific beside

        sea,

        the unknown magic he loves
    throws himself into

        the blue heart.

The poet tells us

> how he feels now
> everything passing through him like light.

He is literally on the edge here, "joyous and breaking down" into the world — yet he remains distinct, intact, within this union. It is not, I think, "suicide into nature." Simple physical sanity (plus humor) is once again his salvation:

> Good
> morning to your body
> hello nipple
> and appendix scar like a letter
> of too much passion
> from a mad Mexican doctor

There is sometimes a lady present, and they live for the moment. Their imaginations interact with America (Kansas and Missouri) and with old movies like *Casablanca*; Ondaatje imagines the Bogart character after the movie's end bitterly regretting the noble renunciation of his lover (Ingrid Bergman). Finally the poet both identifies with and distinguishes himself from Rilke, whom he addresses directly, making reference to the poems of Phyllis Webb (to whom *Tin Roof* is dedicated), and concludes:

> I wanted poetry to be walnuts
> in their green cases
> but now it is the sea
> and we let it drown us,
> and we fly to it released
> by giant catapults
> of pain loneliness deceit and vanity

I'm not sure quite what to make of this conclusion. Obviously the poet accuses himself of certain common human faults, yet these seem to be the mainspring of his surrender to a poetry of the world itself in flux; that is, not a poetry *imposed* on the world, as in the

past. My sense of the whole poem is that, despite the announcement of crisis, there is here a degree of acceptance, though not without "pain" and "loneliness," of the world and self; that is, the poem
embodies that growing sense of balance I have found in the poems
of "Pig Glass," rearranging as it does a number of long-familiar
Ondaatje themes and materials. Crises are also opportunities for
growth.

This is perhaps the place to remind myself and other readers
that Ondaatje's highly developed sense of humor has always provided a certain counterweight to his violent melodrama and to the
Byronic romanticism that causes him to announce from time to
time that he is going crazy or that he feels he may not survive this
or that year or summer. Humor helps to create the complex artistic
balance of *Billy the Kid* and *Coming Through Slaughter*. And in the
shorter poems too it can accompany and to some extent lighten the
grotesque or violent. "Letters and Other Worlds" is one good example of this. In other, non-violent poems Ondaatje makes comic
instead of tragic art from the conflict of intellect and instinct, art
and life as in "The Strange Case":

> My dog's assumed my alter ego.
> Has taken over — walks the house
> phallus hanging wealthy and raw
> in front of guests, nuzzling
> head up skirts
> while I direct my mandarin mood.
>
> Last week driving the baby sitter home.
> She, unaware dog sat in the dark back seat,
> talked on about the kids' behaviour.
> On Huron Street the dog leaned forward
> and licked her ear.
> The car going 40 miles an hour
> she seemed more amazed
> at my driving ability
> than my indiscretion.
>
> It was only the dog I said.

Oh she said.
Me interpreting her reply all the way home.

As we have seen, the notion of "alter ego" is extremely important throughout Ondaatje's work. Here the passionate and reckless "other" Ondaatje is laid not on Billy the Kid or Buddy Bolden or his tragic father but, comically, on the well-hung dog. This leaves the "I" of the poem free to be his more "ordinary" self.

As I suggested in my opening paragraph, some Ondaatje poems have impressed me much more than others. For the record these are: "Paris" (which he chose to discard, leaving it out of his selected poems), "The Diverse Causes," "Peter," "Burning Hills," "We're at the Graveyard," "White Dwarfs," "Walking to Bellrock," and "Light." (A near-miss might be "Letters and Other Worlds," which is certainly thematically central in Ondaatje's work and development, but which I find as rhythmically and grammatically awkward as it is powerful.) To say just why, and examine each of these favorites closely, would take another essay, but I must add that when a contemporary poet has written eight or more poems I admire very much, then his batting average is (with this reader) a good one. Obviously, I "like" numbers of other Ondaatje poems, but these seem to me to be the best — for their qualities of sound, rhythm, diction, and imagery as well as for sensuous immediacy and emotional strength and depth. Ondaatje's work, exploring as it does a psychological reality, does not, I think, have the kind of social or historical or metaphysical scope and range that one finds in the best poems of Al Purdy or Margaret Avison. It *does* have brilliant effects, wonderful immediacy, and impressive emotional depth. Moreover, as the artist has matured, his work has become increasingly relaxed (in the best sense) and accomplished as he has moved beyond shock tactics (or what a witty novelist of my acquaintance has called "special effects") and obvious "layering" or metaphor.

But there is, of course, in all poetry (and civilization) an inevitable and inescapable "layering": we have imposed our own "myth" on the world, on empirical reality, in inventing, using and living within language at all. Thus Italo Calvino (in *The New York Review of Books*, May 12, 1983) writes: "This world I see, the one we ordinarily

recognize as *the* world, presents itself to my eyes — at least to a
large extent — already defined, labeled, catalogued. It is a world
already conquered, colonized by words, a world that bears a heavy
crust of speech." Man is the "language animal" as George Steiner (I
think) once said.

Still, I have believed that poetry at its highest power (which is
language at its highest power) is that musical use of language that
may transcend the apparent limitations as well as the tyranny of
language; that is, it is the language the poet finds both within and
beyond the self, the language that is, in his or her physiological
process of sense-perception, the poet's and the world's together,
words caught and disposed within that larger sound and rhythm of
things that contains poet and external landscape and language alike
as eternally related parts of its ceaseless continuing. More simply,
it is shaped by, even becomes, the rhythm of the organism (mind
and body) interacting with the rhythm of environment/universe:
here metaphor may be important but it is *sound* that is primary. At
his best Michael Ondaatje, a true poet, has been part of that large
flow.

11 Gwendolyn MacEwen's Global Consciousness

1

The extraordinary versatility of Gwendolyn MacEwen is on display yet again in three recent books. *Earthlight* is a new selection of her poems that is independent of *Magic Animals*, the selection that already existed. *Trojan Women* contains MacEwen's new version of Euripides' play and her translations (with Nikos Tsingos) of two long poems by the contemporary Greek poet Yannis Ritsos. In *The T.E. Lawrence Poems* MacEwen assumes the persona of the complex, unhappy man behind the legend of Lawrence of Arabia. Both Euripides and Lawrence are, I think, fairly thoroughly MacEwenized (Lawrence perhaps less so); but Ritsos emerges in English with a voice that has great authority and is quite unlike MacEwen's own.

    Earthlight is a surprisingly good collection. *Magic Animals*, naturally enough, got more of the best early MacEwen poems, but there are some very good ones here too — particularly those with definite occasions or subjects, such as "For Hart Crane" and "One Arab Flute," a superior tourist poem. Often MacEwen combines natural or colloquial speech with rather esoteric symbolism. She is a poet of psychological or inner mystical realities rendered as ecstatic utterance. Obviously, this romantic kind of expression can produce both hits and misses, and some early poems seem cluttered with urgent images and condensed ideas.

"Skulls and Drums" shows the early MacEwen's ease and command:

> you talked about sound, not
> footstep sound, shiphorn, nightcry,
>   but
>
> strings collecting, silver
> and catgut, violas riding
> the waves of May like soft ships,
>   yes
>
> and the anchoring senses,
> the range, the register,
> the index,
>   in the ear, the long
> measure from the drums of our skulls
> to the heart (and its particular tempo);
> the music anchored there, gathered
> in.

This poem dates, I suspect, from MacEwen's residence on the Toronto islands, as does an equally evocative prose poem called "Animal Syllables." In it she writes: "Everything begins, everything is a continuum, everything organizes its death." Here we have MacEwen's vision in a nutshell. Her best poems give rhythmic and imagistic expression to a world in constant movement, an eternal present unfolding in the poem's consciousness.

Trojan Women gives us another poet. Ritsos' "Helen" and "Orestes" make wonderful English poems. I am impressed with these translations without being able to read the originals precisely because this poet's grave, rather stately music is so far removed from MacEwen's own characteristic quick, nervous rhythms. Each poem is a modernization of myth. We find Helen as an old woman grown ugly, haunted by ghosts and abused by her mocking young servants, but now completely disabused of vanity, pride, and the destructive passions of her youth. Her monologue, in which she

speaks of "the pointlessness of fame / the pointlessness and tempo-
rality of every victory," is somewhat Rilkean in flavor; or, if it
resembles anything Canadian, it might be Margaret Avison's "The
Agnes Cleves Papers," but Helen's monologue is much more
straightforward in utterance.

"Orestes" is again rather Rilkean in feeling, at least to this
reader. In his monologue Orestes affirms the pure being of things,
and rejects as irrelevant and meaningless the revenge obsessively
sought by his sister; he nevertheless accepts his destiny at dawn,
entering the myth as we know it.

The Trojan Women is sandwiched in between "Helen" and
"Orestes." This makes thematic (as well as chronological) sense,
since Helen is the chief villain of the piece, but the urgent and at
times even hysterical tone is in sharp contrast to the gravity of the
two monologues. More a recitation than a play (as Michael Ondaatje's
theatrical version of *Billy the Kid* is rather more a recitation than a
play), MacEwen's *Trojan Women* is a sustained attack on war and the
aggressive urge in us all. Lightened with occasional and somewhat
slangy humor, it could be (and most probably was) an emotionally
gripping theatrical experience.

The T.E. Lawrence Poems gives us some of the best poetry that
MacEwen has written in years. The author assumes Lawrence's
persona and all that comes with it: his guilt complex, his hatred of
the flesh, his ambition, his legend-making, his homo-eroticism. It
is an effective impersonation and it becomes the vehicle for sinu-
ous and forceful poems:

> You looked into my eyes, the windows to my soul,
>   and said that because they were blue
> You could see right through them, holes in my skull,
>   to the quiet, powerful sky beyond.

MacEwen has said:

> I enjoy writing when there's an intellectual challenge in
> front of me all the time. I could write an awful lot more
> poetry than I do — you know, mood poetry, descriptive
> poetry. But I don't feel this challenges me enough

intellectually. The Lawrence poems did, though, because I had to work with historical facts and philosophical paradoxes.

This is well said. A lyric poet of any intelligence and sensitivity grows tired, eventually, of writing, over and over, what is essentially the same poem. He or she needs a larger framework, larger forms. These books reveal at least three ways in which MacEwen has sought and found that larger framework.

MacEwen's maturity is perhaps signaled as well by the first book-length study of her work. I suspect that this was a thesis since it, unfortunately, often reads like one. Jan Bartley's *Invocations* is a thematic approach in which numbers of poems are briefly cited, but there is relatively little examination of the best poems as poems. Bartley makes MacEwen seem a more programatic and calculating creator (virtually a myth-machine) than I believe her to be. She makes no attempt to bring her thesis up to date, though she mentions the existence of the Lawrence poems. (Nor does she deal with the *political* implications of "One Arab Flute" in her otherwise quite good discussion of that sequence.)

But the book has virtues as well. There is an account of previous MacEwen criticism. There is an intelligent account of MacEwen's two novels, one that owes a good deal to Frank Davey's previous exposition of the role of alchemy in the poems and novels, but Bartley is able to expand upon his insights. She usefully extends as well Margaret Atwood's observation that the "male muse" is at the center of all of MacEwen's work: it's a pity then that she didn't examine the forms this figure assumes in the Lawrence poems.

Generally speaking, this is a useful book for those teachers and students who may have admired MacEwen's work without very fully understanding the Jungian ideas and world-view that inform it.

1983

2

What follows is, of course, only my perspective. A complex person shows different human possibilities to different people.

I first met her in 1966 when she came to do a reading at Queen's University. That was the year of her first important book, *A Break-fast for Barbarians*. The reading had been arranged by Kim and Michael Ondaatje (just a year before Michael's own first book appeared), so they had me to lunch. We all admired MacEwen's early work. At Kim's prompting I offered to entertain Gwen that afternoon before the evening reading, suggesting that we could walk on the frozen lake (I believe it was February), but she was tired — probably, I realized when I knew her better, from a late night in Toronto — and so replied with mild hauteur, "I've *seen* Lake Ontario before."

Later, when I lived in England, Gwen was one of those who recommended to Macmillan of Canada that they do my first substantial collection of poems. She also sent me a letter at one point, though I still scarcely knew her, saying she might be coming over, and why didn't we go to Stonehenge at the summer solstice (and be Druids together?); an interesting proposal, but then she didn't come.

In 1969, when I had returned, our books came out at once, so we did some readings together. (Her book *The Shadow-Maker* won her a Governor-General's Award.) Thereafter we met many times; her temperament was variable enough that I saw her in bad times and good, but often enough we laughed together. When I complained of a hostile review once she said: "Well, you win some, you lose some." We usually met for lunch or dinner. Less typically, when we temporarily lived near each other in the Annex I took her to see *Star Wars*, which had just opened, one afternoon; we both loved it. And there were numerous other occasions in various parts of Toronto as she moved around. She gave me almost all of her books, including *Afterworlds*; I gave her mine.

The younger Gwendolyn was an intense romantic. In an early poem she wrote: "Oh baby, what hell to be Greek in this country / Without wings, but burning anyway." In that poem she imagined a biker as Icarus crashing into Niagara Falls. Her exotic and sometimes surreal imagination took her to the Middle East, past and present, and to Greece, past and present, to make poems that were both historical and personal; her great love of the 1960s (after her very brief early marriage to Milton Acorn) was an Egyptian student, and she later married a Greek singer. (Unfortunately, she seems to have expected these lovers to be avatars; she wrote, in a happy time: "the god you have loved always / will descend and lie with you in paradise.")

But she also informed me one day in 1969 that the map of Canada over her bed was meant to stimulate "Canadian dreams"; the eloquent poems "Dark Pines Under Water" and "The Discovery" seem also to be expressions of this search for native roots.

Gwendolyn did not usually drink alcohol when she met with me. At some point in the 1970s I came to know (through mutual friends) that she was a secret vodka-drinker; but I don't believe (though I could be wrong) that her alcoholism was active in the late 1960s. I suspect that it may have begun in earnest when her Greek marriage was foundering in the mid-to-late 1970s. She also had a variety of physical ailments from which she may have sought relief in the bottle as well as from other pain-killers; she wasn't a social drinker. So I don't really know when it first got out of hand, since I saw her irregularly, usually in December or July when I was in Toronto. I only *saw* her drunk a very few times, I think in the very late 1970s and early 1980s. On one mildly unpleasant occasion I took her out to dinner (where she continued, until we were served, to be rather obstreperous with the staff, who knew her) so she could sober up and calm down.

When she wrote her wonderful later poems she was not, I believe, drinking. She had been warned by doctors in the early 1980s that this could prove fatal to her fragile system, so she went on the wagon; later she would have — I suppose at times of stress — relapses, but would either recover and pull herself together or collapse, sometimes with seizures, and be hospitalized by friends. There were certainly several of these relapses during the 1980s, but in her sober periods she wrote better than ever; she had been stalled with the T.E. Lawrence material till she went on the wagon. Unfortunately, the relapses seem to have taken her over completely sometime in late-1987; she was again hospitalized, again left as soon as she could, and then resumed the now not-so-secret drinking.

I don't know just when the last act began. She seemed more or less all right when I had lunch with her in July. Her book *Afterworlds* had been receiving rave reviews since the spring, and Gwen remarked, almost apologetically, that I would have noticed that she had made poems (as I had previously done) from Fritjof Capra's *The Tao of Physics*, a book I had given her some years earlier and that we had discussed more than once; I replied, of course, that the ideas as we found them were Capra's first, not mine, and then anybody's to make use of. Few poets are original thinkers, and even as a critic I am usually a synthesizer, though I sometimes point out something obvious that nobody else seems to have noticed.

It was a pleasant sunny day. After a while poet Penn (formerly Penny) Kemp and critic-translator Barbara Godard, who had been at another table, joined us. This was pleasant enough too, and though Gwen went off for a bit on a somewhat intense and peculiar digression about her alleged participation in the reclamation of Toronto's stray cats by an animal rights group — she was passionately fond of cats, to the point of putting out food in the back lanes — she seemed quite in control of her life. She even insisted on paying for lunch because she had been making more money than usual in the last couple of years. (A little later, I'm told, she was blowing it on booze.) I had almost always paid the tab before, of course, since I've had a steady job for twenty-some years; though strictly as a writer I doubt if I earned more (quite possibly I earned less) than Gwendolyn in those years.

I'm sorry to sound a bit academic and priggish — two things Gwen most definitely was not — but it's probably one aspect of my character, and I'm trying to be as honest as possible. I'd like, in retrospect, to be able to say that I was a little uneasy about her that day, but the truth is that I was probably no more uneasy than usual. And she was probably less strange than on some earlier occasions. So I guess the unsimple, unspectacular truth is that I both was and was not (since I was used to her) uneasy. Certainly I didn't *want* her to be going off the deep end again, didn't want to see it. Surely, I felt over the years, she would grow more, not less, stable in time.

We spoke again, quite normally, on the phone after that last lunch; Gwen complained about the heat, as she always did in summer. But I think we were evading each other a little too, in the way old friends sometimes do, and also perhaps, on her part (or even mine, unconsciously), because she may have been drinking again — she didn't like me to know about that. At any rate I never saw her

again. In August-September I was on a three-week writer's delega-
tion to China, and when I got back I was immediately involved in
teaching — as well as getting over bronchitis. I assumed I would
probably see Gwen and other Toronto friends at Christmas-time.
The months were passing quite as quickly as usual.

3

"Eros and Thanatos — they're the same thing."
— Gwendolyn MacEwen to Maggie Helwig

I always thought her imagination was somewhat dangerous as well
as magnificent (and I recall Margaret Atwood once saying to me —
words to this effect, or it's how I took them — that Gwen's yearning for far-off times and places created an imbalance on the side of
"inner" existence or experience); but, of course, this helped to
make her the peculiarly valuable writer she was, and is, and in her
best work, certainly, MacEwen the artist clearly perceived the dangers I had in mind, and even rather wonderfully exploited the tensions thus engendered. She also observed, rightly, that Canadians
were too bound to the ordinary, that there was "a big world" out
there beyond our usual self-imposed boundaries of awareness.

Still. The charm of her travel book *Mermaids and Ikons*
notwithstanding, she found that she could not actually live within
Greek society, even in Toronto, and her actual (as opposed to
mythic) experience of Egypt and the Middle East was even briefer.
What she wanted was for these other worlds and other times to
inform her daily life in Toronto. This was bound to produce some
strain.

Gwendolyn saw art as revelation and prophesy, as an expansion
of consciousness that re-creates the world and helps to create the
self — for poet and reader alike. This is impressively demonstrated
in her best earlier poems. But I can't help but wonder now if there
isn't an immense over-compensation here for feelings of social
"placelessness" and lack of identity. If so, it is perhaps revealing that
she never wrote very directly or confessionally — she was too proud
for that — of her own difficult, inevitably wounding childhood and

youth, of her alcoholic father, who died when she was a teenager, or her schizophrenic mother, who lived out her later life institutionalized, not always knowing who her visiting daughter was. Like the guilt-ridden, humiliated, and fable-making T.E. Lawrence, she wanted a nobler history and reality, a grander self.

"I want to construct a myth," she said. She wanted a radically new (yet, paradoxically, very old) context for a redeemed self. She would be born anew of the universe; and the discovery and exploration of the universe would also be its triumphal re-creation. Thus her typical protagonist is a reality-transformer, by turns winemaker or "dancer in reverse" or swimmer or astronaut or magician, an escape artist who finds the way to a new heaven and earth. Thus her alchemical second Adam "cancels the cosmos," for "in his dance / Worlds expire like tides, in his flaming / dance the nameless cosmos / must await his naming." This is, as much as celebration of a larger, more splendid reality, a kind of revenge on the difficult, particular world of separations and children's aid kidnapping that had hurt her.

She speaks of "a wilful hunger" of the soul. Does she know the dangers of such hunger, such will? In her unjustly neglected novel *King of Egypt, King of Dreams* we can see that she does. For her Akhenaton is a creative visionary who refuses to acknowledge either the dark, potentially evil side of his own nature or the temporal responsibility (life here and now) of his empire. Consequently, these overwhelm him. It is a cautionary tale that dramatizes most effectively the dangers of a monolithic attempt to "purify" the recalcitrant, variegated mixture of good and evil in the world as it always is. Gwendolyn told me at the time of the novel's publication that she thought of Akhenaton as being a fanatic "something like Hitler."

But MacEwen's heretical pharaoh is never, of course, so overtly or obviously evil as Hitler must appear to us now (after his atrocities are known, after the intense adulation of millions has faded away). He is more sympathetic than that. His monotheism is a distortion of reality insofar as God is conceived of only as perfect light. This is the kind of psychic totalitarianism that can be used to justify enormities. Akhenaton, we are told, "never permitted himself to reveal that underworld full of the creeping crawling things like violence or bitterness which all men must contain. He distorted those evils and let them build up within him until they emerged in grotesque, insane disguises." He exemplifies an extreme human possibility like one of Leonard Cohen's saints in *Beautiful Losers* or one of Michael Ondaatje's tragic heroes.

I think it's fair to say that Gwendolyn rarely if ever permitted herself to reveal much of her own dark underworld. On the other hand, the stories of *Noman* and *Noman's Land* propose, not without psychological and aesthetic strain, an integration and even reconciliation of MacEwen's various worlds. (The importance of the word "world" with whatever prefix in her work is too obvious to need much stress.) The mythic in which she finds her altered being will (*must*) be perceived in multicultural Toronto. MacEwen's Arab period and her Greek period are succeeded (really, overlaid) by a "Kanadian" period as she continues to insist that all times and places are one, and that this mystical apprehension of the world as one organism always rearranging itself could lead us to a higher sanity and harmony beyond the senseless violence that has been a chief occupation of the human race throughout the ages. Probably one of Gwendolyn's most valuable legacies to us is precisely this global sort of consciousness and conscience. But I'll return to this a little later.

"Toronto is a carnival." Gwen thought that I had said this to her; I thought she had said it first to me. Another odd overlap that she wrote to me about, before I had read *Noman's Land*, was the demon child in that book who is rather like the child in my own story "T." (Yet we hadn't ever discussed writing about disturbed children, or read each other's stories till they were published.) In her case the child is, I think, like his parents Noman and Kali, a version of herself: the deprived angry side that Noman tames. For Gwendolyn, in her best self, had achieved considerable magnanimity.

I've suggested already why she might identify with T.E. Lawrence, the fabulist whose adventures and semi-fictional memoirs were meant to overcome his shame and over-sensitivity about his origins. This makes for a highly effective cross-gender impersonation — of course, MacEwen's narrative protagonists, who are animus-figures, muses, and self-images, are usually male, as if she felt instinctively that this was where power lay — as well as for some of her finest poetry.

After the artistic triumph of *The T.E. Lawrence Poems* — with Atwood's *Journals of Susanna Moodie*, Ondaatje's *Collected Works of Billy the Kid*, and David Helwig's *Atlantic Crossings* surely the most dramatically successful of the many Canadian historical poem-sequences written since the 1960s — comes *Afterworlds*. It has a retrospective air about it from the title on, and will now, of course, be read as some kind of summing-up. For me, Gwendolyn's prose-poem "The Letter" encapsulates what I find most valuable in her mythmaking for us:

> The light is wandering around inventing everything, and I've entered once again this thing I call World-mind. Let me explain. Under these easy trees I catch sight of an indifferent and wonderfully intelligent world; I think it is the planet itself considering its own experience, its own destiny.... Here, within World-mind, I have access to the past and the future as fluid parts of a conscious whole, a mind that is the planet itself lost in thought. The city becomes all cities, the streets are all streets everywhere; I eavesdrop on a thousand secrets, share a thousand lives. The past and the future are now; nothing is ever lost, and everything exists in a quiet, passionate rightness.

This life-enhancing global consciousness, its passionate rightness, is something much deeper than the wilful hunger of the soul, though not unrelated. It is what might have kept her with us somewhat longer. Though, of course, as her "letter" indicates, she is still with us.

Part Two
Changing Historical News

1 Changing
Historical News

Having become, though rather more slowly than, say, Margaret Atwood or George Bowering or David Helwig, a practitioner of fiction as well as of poetry and criticism, I have been challenged to write a "personal" essay on fiction comparable to my essay on poetry. In that piece I wrote: "It is not merely that the past *lives* and helps to define us now; the act of poetry itself touches upon an eternal now." It seems obvious to me that the first part of this statement has as much to do with the impulse to fiction as it does with the impulse to poetry. But does the second? I'm not sure I know.

I have also written in passing that fiction arises from personal and/or collective reflection on experience, personal and/or collective knowledge and memory. Memory is inescapably selective, though, and thus itself a form of fiction. Many contemporary writers are therefore interested in the blurred boundaries of "fact" and fiction, in the ways in which the mind makes and unmakes its reality. This is a conscious concern of my own third-published novel *Voices on the Brink*.

Authors are now acknowledging that their readers too are constantly "making up" the world. I believe there is a common world, but each organism "knows" it in its own way. The author now acknowledges the reader's creative independence, and may even encourage it (or pretend to encourage it). But the author, however self-consciously he or she engages or challenges the reader, is still in control of the work — the author's organization of language — and still responsible both for the integrity and the interest of the world presented in the work.

A novel offers a "world" to be temporarily absorbed in. This world may purport to be an accurate and detailed picture of an actual place and time, or, at another pole of possibility, it may quite openly present itself as the intensely subjective consciousness of some deeply imagined individual. She or he may even be overtly presented as a version of the author — even though still a selection and arrangement of words. Or a novel may announce itself, though fraudulently I believe, as only an autonomous arrangement of words. Indeed, a novel may present any kind of world-consciousness at all that a reader (even just one reader) is prepared at least temporarily to assent to and live in/with.

Which brings me to my only two "rules" about fiction, or writing in general. The first was given to me (and, I suspect, to lots of other people, though I don't know that she ever put it into print) by Margaret Laurence, who may well, for all I know, have gotten it from someone else. "The writer's first duty," she said, "is not to bore the reader." To which I want to add only: "You can do anything at all that you want to do as long as you can make it work." What does work, when and where and for whom, remains, of course, problematical each time out. But one wants to assume the widest possible latitude for expression rather than feel constricted by received ideas and theories about fiction.

Perhaps, then, I really don't have any (though no doubt each of us begins with some more or less unshakeable and ingrained, partly unconscious assumptions based on past reading and education). Perhaps I have only the sort of intimations suggested above. I don't at this point feel I'd be helped by a highly developed theory. Maybe some day, when I've had a great deal more experience to draw on, though, I'll want to turn into Henry James. Meanwhile, however, my experience of writing six published works of fiction (plus three early failed novels from which I was able to rescue a few parts) has led me, along with my teaching of Canadian and other early twentieth-century and contemporary novels, to reflect a little upon the various particular kinds of fiction that have attracted me.

My debut, *Rosemary Goal*, published in 1978 and republished in 1992, is an academic sex-comedy, more farcical and tolerant in the Canadian way of Leacock, Davies, and others than bitingly satirical, but with a more lyrical though truncated "poet's novel" of love, betrayal, and death embedded within it. This mongrel always made some thematic sense, and at least one rather kind reviewer, Michael Hurley, elaborated upon the pattern of the interwoven works most generously; but the pace of the comedy was so much swifter than that of the lyrical excerpts (which were the remains of one of the aforementioned failed novels, indeed my first attempt at a novel, called *Journey on the Underground*) that the attempt at metafiction (that is, two novels, each written by a character in the other one, though the comedy clearly contains the tragedy rather more than vice versa) somewhat undermined itself. Some might rationalize this as "deconstructive," but my truth is that I was mixing social comedy and the poet's novel rather badly. Still, *Rosemary Goal* has had a few (about ten, I think) ardent fans whom I respect and appreciate. And though it was written in the early 1970s I don't think its social observation has dated much.

If the complete version of *Journey on the Underground* was my first novel, and *Rosemary Goal* proper my second, then my third was an attempt at a heightened chronicle of much that happened personally and nationally between 1966 (with flashbacks to the 1940s) and 1976 (with flash-forward to some distant future). This over-ambitious monster was probably influenced by Hugh MacLennan's national allegories, though his own partly futuristic *Voices in Time* was yet to come when I was writing. My own chronicle or abortive epic was a disaster with a few better moments and stretches. It was too episodic and had far too many characters and was weighed down by being so leadenly though loosely based on my own rather crowded and episodic life. From it, however, I rescued a long story of the late 1960s set in London, England and called "Strawberry Fields"; this appeared in *Glass Houses* (1985), and much later inspired a fictional film which troubles the imagination of the actress-narrator of my fifth-published novel, *Goddess Disclosing*.

From this and my next experience of writing a novel that didn't work I may have learned the hard way the virtues of economy and

dramatic compression in fiction, and also that attempting to uti-
lize one's own recent experience can be dangerously inhibiting to
dramatic invention (at least for me: certainly, quite wonderful
autobiographical novels exist). "Strawberry Fields" recounts a fictional version of experience that had had time to assume an aesthetically ordered shape in memory. (I'm glad I salvaged it for publication, since a short-story writer I greatly respect likes it best
among my fictions.)

My third failure was a sequel to *Rosemary Goal* that carried on
the personal story while making comedy out of Toronto life and
satirizing the Canadian literary scene from coast to coast. This was
a lot of fun to write (and no doubt worked off some of my less char-
itable private feelings about said scene) but the threefold plan did
not make for a coherent novel. Once I had accepted this, I rescued
"The Revenge of Rosemary Goal" and a longer story, "Barbara and
Harold on the Island: an idyll," for *Glass Houses*.

Mention of Harold Brunt, first-person narrator of *Rosemary Goal*
and probably my first very successful creation, reminds me that I
had aspired not only to the lyrical poet's novel, to social comedy,
and to social chronicle but to the novel of character (as practiced by,
say, Margaret Laurence or Mordecai Richler) as well. Integrating
these kinds and qualities of fiction in one work was my problem. It
wasn't so much that I wanted to be Atwood, MacLennan, Laurence,
Findley, Davies, and Richler in one person (just to take some possible Canadian models — I could also cite Joyce, Lawrence, Faulkner,
Virginia Woolf, Lawrence Durrell, Patrick White, and other non-
Canadian models). It was that I wanted a novel with lyricism, comedy, arresting dialogue, social and historical significance, and the
emotional force of character rendered in depth. I also wanted it to
have the advantages of both first- and third-person narration.

My next real stab at all of this in one coherent form is *Adele at
the End of the Day* (1987). It was written with relatively little
strain or trouble between 1983 and 1985. But first, in 1978, I had
begun another novel, my fifth (if you're still counting), at least in
its first version. It was an attempt to deal with the time and place
of my childhood and youth in the 1940s, 1950s, and early 1960s;
that is, the sort of lyrical growing-up novel that is often the
author's first. I also wanted to address large social and ecological

concerns. But my first draft, a fairly short novel completed in 1982, seemed maddeningly incomplete and not wholly coherent to those who read it (such are the joys of apprenticeship). A young friend eventually put it most succinctly: "It's too short for what it's saying." So I eventually put it aside, but later rewrote it as *Voices on the Brink* (1989). The "brink" is Niagara, my native place.

When the idea for *Adele* came it was late one afternoon at Christmastime of 1982 in the bar at the top of Toronto's Park Plaza Hotel. I realized that this was what I must do next (while various publishers were taking their time, as is their wont, in rejecting number 5). But I couldn't effectively begin till spring because I was still teaching a full load. Then the two main characters, mother and son, and the plot of their parallel lives in two generations seemed to unfold and flow gradually, sometimes surprisingly but always steadily for the two years, interrupted by teaching, that the writing took.

I can't yet (if ever) judge this work objectively, but I think I did to some degree put together successfully the disparate qualities of my previous, less mature fictions. I also enjoyed moving rapidly and frequently between first and third persons, and past and present tenses. And it is perhaps a good lesson for me that *Adele*, my most critically applauded fiction to date, is the one furthest from my own life. A number of very favorable reviews, especially (and this is rather marvelous luck) in *The Globe and Mail* and *The New York Times* (since this was also the first of my fictions to find publication abroad), confirmed my feeling that I must have learned something about the craft.

In 1985-86 I wrote in one year — having by now become so addicted to the solitary vice of fiction as to reduce my teaching load and thus lower my income — my longest novel yet. This was later rewritten to become *Changelings* (1991). *Changelings* has been advertised as a "psychological thriller"; it's an exploration of the phenomenon of multiple personality. *Voices on the Brink*, for its part, has elements of autobiography (bits and pieces) and of the poet's mystery novel.

Which brings me back to the question of kinds of novels. In the fall of 1988 I taught a graduate half-course of my own devising on the Canadian poet's novel. Since I was a poet first myself it's possible that I'm particularly susceptible to such novels. Certainly I have been excited as well by such foreign examples as *The White Hotel*, and was rather amused when one of the few reviewers hostile to *Adele* announced sniffily that she was offended for similar reasons by D.M. Thomas's splendidly imaginative and powerfully compassionate work.

From our class discussions there emerged several main ideas about Canadian poet's novels: that they are often "mystery" stories that investigate something hidden or denied (for example, *The Double Hook, The Second Scroll, Surfacing, Noman's Land, Coming Through Slaughter*, David Helwig's *The Bishop*, Joy Kogawa's *Obasan*); that "magic" and some larger, religious mystery are often involved; that these books are, as I wrote in *Harsh and Lovely Land*, "quests into darkness"; that sometimes the darkness is identified with Canada (or for Gwendolyn MacEwen "Kanada"); that often the novels "re-vision" history (for example, *The Second Scroll, Beautiful Losers, Obasan*, George Bowering's *Burning Water*); that these novels display a minority sensibility and perspective(s) that are subversive of majority "norms" and assumptions.

This last observation is perhaps worth expanding. Here a useful point of departure is *Beautiful Losers*, in which Leonard Cohen's "F." wants to be the Moses or Messiah for all "orphans": Québécois, Indians, Blacks, "New Jews," homosexuals, junkies, and etc. *The Second Scroll* deals, of course, with the Jewish people at large, and with the hybrid Jewish-Canadian state of being, as well as with the clash of cultures in and out of Canada. *Noman's Land* presents multicultural Toronto, and even manages to incorporate Grey Owl the fake Indian into its myth of the "Kanadian" identity. *Coming Through Slaughter* gives us Black jazz musicians, and *In the Skin of a Lion* exploited immigrant workers in Toronto. *Obasan* speaks eloquently of the story of Japanese-Canadians; *Burning Water* examines the clash of Indian, English, Spanish, and American cultures, adding a homosexual note to the traditional "facts" about the adventures of Captain George Vancouver. Even Sheila Watson's *The Double Hook* gives us a geographically isolated, marginal community (as does her earlier novel *Deep Hollow Creek*, not published till 1992); Douglas LePan's highly charged fable *The Deserter* focuses on deserters and outcasts wandering in a dark underworld; and

Elizabeth Smart's *By Grand Central Station I Sat Down and Wept* is a long lyric cry of exile. Some of these books have prominent feminist themes or implications. In all of this the multiplicity of Canada, a collection of minorities in which everyone is in some way "dark" and "other," is reflected.

How much bearing any or all of this has on my own fictions I must leave to others to decide. I think, some. My fifth-published novel, *Goddess Disclosing* (1992), probably is the most obvious candidate for poem-novel, since it consists of lyrical monologues for Gaia. But while the poet's novel has greatly intrigued me, I would not want to feel I was confined to such a category. For I have always been interested in the evolution of various kinds of novels that have emerged from the Canadian experience, as another essay in this book on the traditions of comic and historical fiction should make clear.

Is it useful to reiterate, finally, that fiction gives us the always-changing historical news while poetry at its purest touches on an eternal now? The narrative poems and poetic novels of such as Atwood, MacEwen, Ondaatje, and Helwig do rather blur the distinction. And perhaps this fruitful confusion is as far as I, "personally," have gotten.

I suspect, though, that in future I might still want to argue that fiction tells us where we've been, and what *this* is becoming, while the heightened sound and rhythm of poetry (sometimes found, of course, within a novel) embodies our deepest, most mysterious being.

2 Balance and Perspective:
Stephen Leacock's *Sunshine Sketches*

It seems inevitable that sensitive Canadians will have a shifting perspective on reality. The land may well be a sleeping giant, but the political and social nation has often enough been a dwarf in giant's robes. And I believe it is Stephen Leacock's Canadian vision of a world that is constantly changing its shape that elevates *Sunshine Sketches of a Little Town* to the level of a minor masterpiece in world literature.

Leacock himself lived an exemplary version of the Canadian paradox: a boy from the bush, he was also from a genteel English family. His father was a remittance man and a drunk, and his mother a type of Mrs. Moodie incongruously keeping up standards as best she could in the wilderness. Their ambitious son celebrated the simple life in nature, yet craved (and got) fame, status, and money to compensate for the miseries of his childhood and youth. Some of his political and social opinions are obnoxious in the extreme, yet there is a real wisdom in his work, an insight into the nature of Canadian existence as shrewd as that of any writer who has spoken to us since.

Leacock's Mariposa, itself a microcosm of the English Canadian nation of almost a century ago, is a community located on the edge of a vast wilderness:

Outside of Mariposa there are farms that begin well but get thinner and meaner as you go on, and end sooner or later in bush and swamp and the rock of the north country. And beyond that again, as the background of it all, though it's far away, you are somehow aware of the great pine woods of the lumber country reaching endlessly into the north.

And one's perception of Mariposa is decidedly determined by one's shifting perspective:

Of course if you come to the place fresh from New York, you are deceived. Your standard of vision is all astray. You do think the place is quiet. . . . But live in Mariposa for six months or a year and then you will begin to understand it better; the buildings get higher and higher; the Mariposa House grows more and more luxurious; McCarthy's Block towers to the sky; the buses roar and hum to the station; the trains shriek; the traffic multiplies; the people move faster and faster.

Leacock presents the *Mariposa Belle* in similar terms:

The Mariposa Belle always seems to me to have some of those strange properties that distinguish Mariposa itself. I mean, her size seems to vary so. If you see her there in the winter, frozen in the ice beside the wharf with a snowdrift against the windows of the pilot house, she looks a pathetic little thing the size of a butternut. But in the summer time, especially after you've *been* in Mariposa for a month or two, and have paddled alongside her in a canoe, she gets larger and taller, and with a great sweep of black sides, till you see no difference between the *Mariposa Belle* and the *Lusitania*.

Later, the *Belle* is a floating cross-section of Mariposa (or Canada) itself. Here the reference to the seasons reminds us of another aspect of the shifting Canadian reality. In summer things

open out and enlarge themselves; in winter they close in upon
themselves and diminish. "There never was such a place," Leacock
writes, "for changing its character with the season." It is all very
well for our literary and cultural critics to speak of liberation from
the mental and social garrison at some times; it is less appropriate
at others. For the land imposes a dual physical and psychic rhythm.
There is a time of hibernation and concealment, and another time
of openness and "jailbreak." Here, of course, the primary emphasis
is on summer.

Out of necessity, the Mariposans have an instinctive awareness
of these things. Their minds are limited but flexible. Like Frank
Scott's Mackenzie King, they never let their "on the one hand"
know what their "on the other hand" is doing. Almost everyone,
we are told, belongs to everything. They are both Liberal and Tory,
British and American. And, Leacock suggests, they are lucky. When
the *Mariposa Belle* sinks to the strains of "*O Ca - na - da*" no real
harm is incurred because of the lucky smallness of things: the
water is less than six feet deep. Here the natural environment, represented by the lake, is reduced in size and made less menacing, as
if the land's menace were only illusion, itself a trick of perspective
like those Leacock perpetrates here and elsewhere in *Sunshine
Sketches*. Indeed, this comic technique might be regarded as thoroughly sentimental, were it not for the intimations of life's harsh-
ness and human tragedy that we find elsewhere in the book. Like
the early A.M. Klein of *Hath Not A Jew . . .* (with its diminutive
idyllic world of dwarfs, children, homunculi, and elves balancing
the more sombre atrocities of Jewish history), Leacock appears at
times to suggest that life on a smaller scale has (or, at any rate, had)
its charms and advantages, and also that Mariposa can be seen as
the Canadian nation in miniature, a small place whose pretensions
and fantasies and vices are comic because ineffectual, and whose
real values are imposed by a lucky smallness — a leaky ship of
state that can come to no real grief.

The matter of scale and perspective is introduced in the first
pages of *Sunshine Sketches*. The *Mariposa Belle* is described in the
second paragraph as "a steamer that is tied to the wharf with two
ropes of about the same size as they use on the *Lusitania*." The
town itself has "to the eye of discernment a perfect jostle of public

institutions comparable only to Threadneedle Street or Lower Broadway." Humor is generated at once by a dual perspective. It is, of course, absurd to the outsider that a place so marginal as Mariposa should be comparable to London and New York, but it is not absurd to the Mariposans. There is a sense, one feels, in which their "eye of discernment" has a rightness of its own.

"The Speculations of Jefferson Thorpe" tends to reinforce one's sense of the good fortune of the Mariposans. The town's barber, whose shop has a prominent "false front," is also an armchair financier. When a mining boom gets underway in the north, he is carried along by the town's excitement, as is everyone except Josh Smith, who knows and dislikes the north, and who prefers to sell potatoes to the miners than to speculate in shares. In the course of the chapter Thorpe acquires $40,000 from his investment in a mine, loses it to swindlers in New York, and is then reduced once more to giving shaves and raising chickens to pay his debts. Throughout, the Mariposans are depicted as fools aping what they understand to be the ways of the city, longing to conform to the urban material standards of the American dream, yet possessing, by luck, another and better standard without really knowing it. Leacock's satire eventually gives way, as it usually does, to pathos, and then to final affirmation:

> Pathetic? tut! tut! You don't know Mariposa. Jeff has to work pretty late, but that's nothing — nothing at all if you've worked hard all your lifetime . . . Anyway, things are not so bad. You see it was just at this time that Mr. Smith's caff opened and Mr. Smith came to Jeff's Woman and said he wanted seven dozen eggs a day, and wanted them handy, and so the hens are back, and more of them, and they exult so every morning over the eggs they lay that if you wanted to talk of Rockefeller in the barber shop you couldn't hear his name for the cackling.

So much for the city. It is significant here that Smith comes to the rescue as he always does in times of crisis; he is the Mariposans' natural leader, a man whose self-interest usually coincides with the interest of the community. This seems to be one principle of Leacock's pragmatic conservatism.

There follows the famous chapter in which Smith saves the day
by patching up the leaking *Mariposa Belle*. In some ways, one is led
to reflect, this wily savior of the Mariposan ship of state, this universal handyman, resembles Leacock's political hero, Sir John A.
Macdonald. He is often crooked in method but usually beneficent in
over-all intent. Equally significant in this chapter, however, is the
introduction of Dean Drone, who ought to be Smith's complement.

Drone is, to the extent of his meager talents, the guardian of
the moral and imaginative life of the community. On the cruise of
the *Mariposa Belle* we find him conversing at cross-purposes with
Dr. Gallagher. Gallagher is obsessed with Canadian history and
native relics, Drone with classical Greek history and culture.
Gallagher is a Liberal, Drone a Conservative. The native culture
and the European cultural past seem here to be quite irrecon-
cileable; at any rate, neither of these men is capable — as some of
our early poets were — of the imaginative leap that might see parallel energies and myths at work in them. Cruising on the
Mariposa Belle, Drone and Gallagher represent two worlds that do
not fuse:

> Dr. Gallagher said that if Dean Drone would come round to
> his house some night he would show him some Indian arrow
> heads that he had dug up in his garden. And Dean Drone said
> that if Dr. Gallagher would come round to the rectory any
> afternoon he would show him a map of Xerxes' invasion of
> Greece. Only he must come some time between the Infant
> Class and the Mothers' Auxiliary.
>
> So presently they both knew that they were blocked out of
> one another's houses for some time to come, and Dr.
> Gallagher walked forward and told Mr. Smith, who had
> never studied Greek, about Champlain crossing the rock
> divide.
>
> Mr. Smith turned his head and looked at the divide for half
> a second and then said he had crossed a worse one up north
> back of the Wahnipitae and that the flies were Hades — and
> then went on playing freezeout poker with the two juniors
> in Duff's bank.

Smith is, of course, indifferent to Gallagher's history (and undoubtedly totally unconcerned about anything Greek), since he is a doer, not a dreamer.

Drone and Gallagher are briefly juxtaposed and contrasted, but both are dreamers; the more important pair of opposites is, of course, Smith and Drone. Their contrasted temperaments, concerns, and values reveal a basic structural principle in *Sunshine Sketches*: the delicate balance between hard reality and imagination as determining factors in human life and behavior; between the claims of economics and politics on the one hand and our cultural and spiritual life on the other; between a pragmatic materialism and the magic represented all too inadequately by Drone's fading memory of Greek culture; between outer and inner worlds.

George Grant, in his essay "In Defence of North America," included in *Technology and Empire*, has written eloquently of some of the problems touched upon here:

> Living undivided from one's own earth: here is not only a form of living which has not been ours but which is named in a language the echoes of which are far from us. The remoteness of "chthonic" from us measures our separation from Europe. Greece lay behind Europeans as a first presence; it has not so lain for us. It was for them primal in the sense that in its perfected statements educated Europeans found the way things are. The Greek writings bared a knowledge of the human and non-human things which could be grasped as firmness by the Europeans for the making of their own lives and cities. Most important, Plato and Aristotle presented contemplation as the height for man.
>
> . . . . .
>
> When we go to the Rockies we may have the sense that gods are there. But if so, they cannot manifest themselves to us as ours. They are the gods of another race, and we cannot know them because of what we are and what we did. There can be nothing immemorial for us except the environment

as object. Even our cities have been encampments on the
road to economic mastery.

Neither the Greek nor the Indian magic, Grant feels, is accessible
to us. Not all our writers are so pessimistic. John Newlove and
Margaret Atwood are only two among recent poets who have
sought a relationship with the gods of place, and Leonard Cohen
has suggested a poetic analogy between ancient, presumably
Dionysian Greeks and Indians. But Leacock, one feels, would agree
with Grant. For Josh Smith, who sees the "environment as
object," is more important to the Mariposans than Gallagher or
Drone.

Dean Drone, though depicted as a kind of saintly idiot or child,
retains some vestigial sense of the value of the contemplation of
"human and non-human things," but it serves only to isolate him
more and more from the community for which he should act as
guide. Part of his problem is that he seems, like many a fool-saint,
blind to the nature of the world immediately about him and to its
possible connection with the imaginative world in which he seems
to spend most of his time. Long ago he took a gold medal in Greek,
but did not learn mathematics; here, as in *Arcadian Adventures
With the Idle Rich*, Leacock appears to suggest that the traditional
classical education which he himself received is, alas, of no practical use in the modern technological society of North America, for
the reasons which George Grant analyzes in his essay. One must,
however regretfully, learn a hard pragmatism in order to survive:
thus Leacock's apparent contempt for poets, ministers, or anyone
else engaged with the inner world, with manifestations of the "spiritual" or "mystical." (Is it possible that he was afraid of something
in himself, something that hard circumstances encouraged him to
suppress? Where does he stand on the relative value of the humani-
ties and the technical skills? On both sides? It is one of my own
beliefs that all artists, even those who profess and who consciously
believe themselves to be rationalists, have a strong streak of the
"mystical" in them, however much they may wish to deny it even
to themselves. In any case, Leacock's characteristic manner is
irony, and it is frequently generated by the conflicting demands of
the "ideal" and the "real.")

The story of the new church which occupies three chapters of *Sunshine Sketches* is full of ironies. The Dean wants to "kindle a Brighter Beacon"; he gets his wish with a vengeance. The new church is to be a "Greater Evidence," but of what?

> . . . from the open steeple of it, where the bells were, you could see all the town lying at its feet, and the farmsteads to the south of it, and the railway like a double pencil line, and Lake Wissanotti spread out like a map. You could see and appreciate things from the height of the new church — such as the size and the growing wealth of Mariposa — that you never could have seen from the little stone church at all.

But as the church falls into debt, the townfolk discover that they are dissatisfied with its conduct, and even doubtful about points of theology enunciated there. An absurd whirlwind campaign fails to raise the necessary funds to encourage a revival of faith, and the Dean determines to resign. Here the theme of the "buried life" or what might be called the "mute inglorious Milton" motif is introduced:

> I believe that at the time when Rupert Drone had taken the medal in Greek over fifty years ago, it was only a twist of fate that had prevented him from becoming a great writer. There was a buried author in him just as there was a buried financier in Jefferson Thorpe. In fact, there were many people in Mariposa like that, and for all I know you may yourself have seen such elsewhere. For instance, I am certain that Billy Rawson, the telegraph operator at Mariposa, could easily have invented radium. In the same way, one has only to read the advertisements of Mr. Gingham, the undertaker, to know that there is still in him a poet, who could have written on death far more attractive verses than the Thanatopsis of Cullen Bryant . . .

Provincial Canada has presumably been packed with potential artists — newspaper editors, teachers, and plowmen — who come to tragicomic ends.

The last of Dean Drone's self-esteem is lost when he finds himself, in a passage that is funny and sad and penetrating at once,
quite unable to compose even a letter of resignation: "the Dean
saw that he was beaten, and he knew that he not only couldn't
manage the parish but couldn't say so in proper English, and of the
two, the last was the bitterer discovery." To this has the tradition
of Christian humanism fallen.

But the day is saved as the church is burned down by Josh
Smith. Because of the Dean's ignorance of mathematics, the
church is heavily over-insured. Thus his incompetence comes to
his rescue: he lives in a comic universe. No one remarks that, to
borrow a phrase from the American military, "we had to destroy
the church in order to save it," but the irony is heavy. A new
church is built from the ashes of the old.

Meanwhile, the sight of the "Brighter Beacon" has caused Dean
Drone to suffer a stroke. The "happy" ending to his story reveals,
moreover, that Leacock's comic vision contains within itself intimations of the tragic sense, and is, in fact, profoundly ambivalent:

> Dean Drone? Did he get well again? Why, what makes you
> ask that? You mean, was his head at all affected after the
> stroke? No, it was not. Absolutely not. It was not affected in
> the least, though how anybody who knows him now in
> Mariposa could have the faintest idea that his mind was in
> any way impaired by the stroke is more than I can tell. The
> engaging of Mr. Uttermost, the curate, whom perhaps you
> have heard preach in the new church, had nothing whatever
> to do with Dean Drone's head. It was merely a case of the
> pressure of overwork. It was felt very generally by the
> wardens that, in these days of specialization, the rector was
> covering too wide a field, and that if he should abandon
> some of the lesser duties of his office, he might devote his
> energies more intently in the Infant Class. That was all. You
> may hear him there any afternoon, talking to them, if you
> will stand under the maple trees and listen through the open
> windows of the new Infant School.
>
> And, as for audiences, for intelligence, for attention —
> well, if I want to find listeners who can hear and understand
> about the great spaces of Lake Huron, let me tell of it, every
> time face to face with the blue eyes of the Infant Class, fresh

from the infinity of spaces greater still. Talk of grown-up
people all you like, but for listeners let me have the Infant
Class with their pinafores and their Teddy bears and their
feet not even touching the floor, and Mr. Uttermost may
preach to his heart's content of the newer forms of doubt
revealed by the higher criticism.

So you will understand that the Dean's mind is, if
anything, even keener, and his head even clearer than
before. And if you want proof of it, notice him there beneath
the plum blossoms reading in the Greek: he has told me that
he finds that he can read, with the greatest ease, works in
the Greek that seemed difficult before, because his head is
so clear now.

And sometimes — when his head is very clear — as he sits
there reading beneath the plum blossoms he can hear them
singing beyond, and his wife's voice.

Here the concepts of space and clarity are relative to one's mental
perspective. More simply: either Dean Drone is crazy (senile, anyhow), or else he is in a state of grace, or else both things are true at
once. It all depends upon one's perspective. Leacock shifts from comedy to pathos, and it might be said that his microcosmic view
domesticates tragedy. (One might consider alongside Dean Drone's
stroke the suicide of young Fizzlechip and the death of Neil
Pepperleigh, but these incidents are passed over relatively quickly.)
What does Leacock really think about the story of Dean Drone?
At times in this book and in *Arcadian Adventures* he seems to be
extraordinarily cynical. Does he believe that the character and
methods of a Smith are absolutely necessary to the survival of
human society? The whole story of Dean Drone involves the conflict of material and spiritual realities; it seems to me likely that
this is a tension within Leacock himself; that is, he is on both
sides. In any case, a principle of balance is maintained throughout
Sunshine Sketches. The story of Dean Drone, who could not reconcile or fuse the ideal and the real (and is thus left in more or less
isolated communion with the ideal) is followed by the sentimental
and absurd love story of Peter Pupkin and Zena Pepperleigh, who
can. The slightly sticky conclusion to their story is then balanced
by the satiric bite of the chapters on the stormy "reciprocity" election of 1911. The "Envoi" puts the whole into a final perspective.

Zena Pepperleigh is, like Dean Drone, a dreamer, but her dreams are less refined than those of the Dean. Again, ironies abound. Zena's ideas of the heroic lover are taken from ridiculous historical romances, while her father's notion of the hero comes from *The Life of Sir John A. Macdonald* and *Pioneer Days in Tecumseh Township* (here the traditional, in the form of European romance, and the native are again juxtaposed and contrasted); Pupkin manages to satisfy both criteria. Zena dreams of a prince under a spell, and in a sense Pupkin is just that, since he is concealing the fact that his family is rich. Pupkin feels that his pursuit of Zena is nearly hopeless, but in fact their fathers are old friends, and the match is pre-ordained — possibly even plotted and manipulated. But the pair are genuinely "in love," however ridiculous love's manifestations to the outsider, and love triumphs. In all of this (leaving aside the rather tedious burlesque of the attempted "bank robbery," itself a small story about illusion and reality) there is a complicated play of romance, satire on romance (in all of the overlapping senses of the word), and some final fusion. To the outsider Pupkin is a silly, and it is more than hinted, rather stupid young man, but to Zena he is an enchanted prince: both perspectives remain valid.

In the chapters dealing with the election we are faced once again with the Mariposans as a community in action. We learn that everybody in town is "either a Liberal or a Conservative or else is both," and we are introduced to John Henry Bagshaw, the sitting Liberal member, and to Edward Drone, "a somewhat weaker copy of his elder brother" who sets out to run as an independent on a platform of honesty and public morality: perhaps Leacock is prophesying the pieties of third parties to come. The Conservatives have, inevitably, nominated Josh Smith who sets out effectively to be all things to all people, and even embraces temporarily a platform of "temperance and total prohibition."

On election day each candidate is declared the victor in turn. But it develops that most of the voters are waiting till the eleventh hour to jump on the bandwagon and vote for the apparent winner. Knowing this, Smith ensures his victory by wiring to the city news of his triumph, which is then wired back to Mariposa. Thus the Mariposans receive their instructions to elect Smith. It seems that half an hour is a long time in politics.

In the "Envoi" Leacock bids farewell to his reader. We learn here for the first time that not only the narrator but also the reader came long ago from Mariposa: narrator and reader are now sitting in the Mausoleum Club in the city, having left the enchanted town behind. The reader is implicated in this betrayal and loss.

But there is a train that goes from the city to the suburbs and then "turns itself little by little into the Mariposa train thundering and pounding towards the north with hemlock sparks pouring out into the darkness from the funnel of it." Its size and importance increase as it moves toward Mariposa. This train journey is a journey into the past, to an older, simpler world. (The future, the shape of things to come, is examined in *Arcadian Adventures*.) Now it is autumn, not summer.

> How fast the train goes this autumn night! You have travelled, I know you have, in the Empire State Express, and the New Limited and the Maritime Express that holds the record of six hundred whirling miles from Paris to Marseilles. But what are they to this, this mad career, this breakneck speed, this thundering roar of the Mariposa local driving hard to its home! Don't tell me that the speed is only twenty-five miles an hour. I don't care what it is. I tell you, and you can prove it for yourself if you will, that that train of mingled flat cars and coaches that goes tearing into the night, its engine whistle shrieking out its warning into the silent woods and echoing over the dull still lake, is the fastest train in the whole world.
>
> Yes, and the best too.

Finally there is the cry of the brakemen and the porters: "*MARI-POSA! MARIPOSA!*"

> And, as we listen, the cry grows fainter and fainter in our ears and we are sitting here again in the leather chairs of the Mausoleum Club, talking of the little Town in the Sunshine that once we knew.

An infinite pathos is created. For Leacock is, one senses, committed to both lives. Life on a smaller scale is, he suggests, more humane, less mechanical. But it is in the nature of man to be ambitious, to seek wealth and fame, to be driven to destroy or neglect that which, finally, he values most. Leacock's view of human nature is cause for a great sadness; he tells the reader (and himself?): "Your face has changed in these long years of money-getting in the city. Perhaps if you had come back now and again, just at odd times, it wouldn't have been so." One hopes that he could go back (and I mean, of course, more than the physical return to Orillia), that he achieved a dual rhythm.

This book, one of the world's minor masterpieces, is also one of the most "Canadian" ever written. Leacock has given us a vision of Canada, at least as it was: a place of small communities whose pretensions are comic and whose real values are imposed by the luck of smallness. But this picture was incomplete even then, as he well knew, without the complementary and more sinister portrait of the city, which he was to sketch so vividly in *Arcadian Adventures with the Idle Rich*.

3 Tragic Ambivalence:
The Novels of Morley Callaghan

Morley Callaghan takes the Canadian novel into the tangled web of the city. Like Stephen Leacock, he is inclined to be ambivalent about what he finds there. *Such is My Beloved*, the first novel of his artistic maturity, presents us with a world in which it is difficult to know what is illusion and what is reality, or whether madness and divinity are distinguishable; it is a world where the Marxist may be the better Christian and where prostitutes may be seen as priests and the Church as a prostitute.

There is irony and ambivalence even in the structure of Callaghan's best novels: his style is naturalistic — it is a style akin to that of his one-time friend Ernest Hemingway, a style that embodies in its steady meat-and-potatoes accumulation of "just the facts" the naturalistic philosophy of biological and social determinism found in, say, *A Farewell to Arms* (or in Frederick Philip Grove's novels, for that matter) — but his overall strategy is symbolic parable or allegory, and thus suggests another world, a transcendent spiritual reality and an inner freedom that is independent of outward social circumstances. Which vision of existence, the reader may ask, does Callaghan believe to be true? Or is it that both are true at once, as truths belonging to two orders, that is, to an earthly plane and to the larger perspective that ultimately contains it? We are left pretty much unenlightened in the early novels. It may be that there is a larger reality, but the possibility is only raised, not definitely confirmed. The "spiritual" might only be illusion, a trick of the pattern-making brain, after all.

This is, at any rate, the way in which I read the best earlier novels. I rather suspect, judging from what he has said in interviews, that Callaghan may not agree with me, but I prefer, not without misgivings about my own brashness, to trust the tale. It tends to be the same tale told over and over for many years. But there is a turning point after which it acquires somewhat greater plausibility.

Such Is My Beloved, in which an idealistic priest befriends and attempts to help two prostitutes, is the first novel to pose the problem clearly. It is dedicated to the Catholic theologian Jacques Maritain, who apparently provided Callaghan with a counterweight to Hemingway's naturalistic pessimism. Maritain's philosophy of "personalism" proposes (among other things) the possibility of an individual who has an inner peace and integrity that makes him or her spiritually and morally independent of the compromises and hypocrisies of society. Such an individual may come into conflict with society and even be destroyed by it, but he or she will triumph spiritually. Callaghan's novels explore this possibility. But what do they conclude?

Consider the way in which the first three chapters of *Such Is My Beloved* end:

> . . . he was so moved that when he got into bed he felt that his feeling for the girls was so intense it must surely partake of the nature of divine love.

> Then suddenly he wondered if he ought to have given them money. He tried to define the objection to giving them money, but it remained too deeply hidden within him.

> "He [Father Dowling] would have been glad to see how I chased that little college boy out of the room," she [Midge] thought, smiling. There would have been something about it that would have pleased him. It was almost as though she had done something for him, and it was more likely that he would give her money the next time he came to the hotel.

The objection to giving the girls money is surely this: that Father Dowling is buying the attention, affection, companionship, and temporary good-behavior of the two girls just as other men buy their bodies. He feels that his emotional attachment to the girls partakes of the nature of divine love, and perhaps it does, but we are also shown that this man is so impoverished in the realm of personal attachments that he is jealous of his only real friend's fiancée. He is a man whose ardent nature, as expressed in his sermons, has had no immediate and personal object before his encounter with the prostitutes. But how could he love them, he asks eventually, except personally? This involves an intense and difficult relationship, since Father Dowling has no intention of allowing his quite conscious sexual desire to interfere with his priestly vows and vocation. He is aroused by Midge, is perhaps even in love with her, and he is stimulated to erotic dreams by his association with the girls, but his determination to help them as friend and priest is not lessened by this temptation.

Still, a conflict is set up within Father Dowling, and it is this, presumably, that accounts for his sudden descent into madness when the girls are put beyond his reach by his disapproving bishop. He has begun to see the girls as the true priests, and the Church as prostitute; the logic of this insight would lead him eventually to deny the value of his celibacy, but this is a step that he is not consciously prepared to take. Because he desperately needs to resolve the problem of the relationship between carnal and divine love, however, he turns to the highly erotic but sanctified Song of Songs for guidance. (Nowadays, of course, he might well leave the priesthood and marry Midge instead.)

Father Dowling is obliged, because of his training and conscious convictions, to rationalize his love for Midge by idealizing her:

> . . . he really loved the way she was apt to burst out laughing, as if the faintest incident touched her deeply, as if the sensation of the most fleeting moment had to be savored fully. "That attitude in her is really Christian in the best sense of the word," he thought. "That desire to make each moment precious, to make the immediate eternal, or rather to see the eternal in the immediate."

And she was watching him lazily, thinking, "If he keeps
on staying, I won't be able to go out. What does he want to
say? There's something on his mind. He's a very nice man.
Maybe I don't really want to go out. Maybe I could get him
to come over here and sit beside me."

Callaghan's complexity can be sampled here. Perhaps Father
Dowling's reverence for Midge is justified, even though she would
never think in such terms. Perhaps if she succeeded in making him
sit beside her, and things proceeded further, he might discover in a
deeper way "the eternal in the immediate." And then again, perhaps not. All we are allowed to know of her is that she is concerned
about the possible loss of that night's earnings and would like to
seduce Father Dowling because he is "a nice man." Her concerns
are economic and sexual, his ideal: two conceptions of reality are
presented. Can they really be reconciled?

Later on, while hearing the confession of a boy who has been to
a local prostitute, Father Dowling decides quite arbitrarily that it
"was probably Midge" and, realizing "how united was all the life
of his congregation, students, the mothers and fathers of students,
prostitutes, priests, the rich and the poor who passed girls on the
street and desired them," he feels that there may be some purpose
in the girls' lives after all; he sits afterwards "smelling the odors of
stale face-powder, cheap perfumes, the mixed breath of many
strangers, the smell of bodies confined in that small space, and as
he listened, it all seemed good to him, like the teeming richness of
living things."

To love the simple and the physical, even the tawdry, must be,
he realizes, the nature of divine love, of loving things and people
for themselves. Even commercial sexuality might be seen as an
expression and vehicle of divine love. Father Dowling feels that
his love for the girls brings him closer to others whom society has
neglected and driven to despair. He tells his Marxist friend Charlie
that prostitution is not merely an economic problem but that the
girls' lives have "in a way . . . a spiritual value":

> These girls were taking on themselves all those mean secret
> passions, and in the daytime those people who had gone to
> them at night seemed to be leading respectable and good lives.

> Those girls never suspect the sacrifice of their souls that they
> offer every day.

The girls are not only, he feels, sacrificial victims of a hypocritical
and corrupt society; they are themselves priests ministering to
others, even Christ-figures:

> Father Dowling suddenly wondered if it could be that the
> bodies of Midge and Ronnie were being destroyed, as the
> bread and wine in the mass would be destroyed, so that God
> could enter in in the mystery of transubstantiation. "The
> death of Christ, the life of souls," he thought.

They are vessels of spirit, then, demonstrating, to Dowling's satisfaction anyhow, that the lowliest of human creatures can contain
divinity even in their lowliest acts (an insight embodied as well in
Adele Wiseman's second novel *Crackpot*).
     Carnality then can be divinity:

> He read with his face beginning to glow; he seemed to
> understand more deeply every passionate avowal of love.
> "We have a little sister with no breasts, what shall we do for
> our little sister?" he read, and he smiled. "At night on my
> bed I sought her whom my soul loveth. . . ." It seemed to
> Father Dowling as he sat at his desk with the city noises of
> that spring night coming through the window that he
> understood this love song as it had never been understood
> before, that each verse had a special, fresh, new meaning for
> him. "I'll write a commentary on it verse by verse and show
> how human love may transcend all earthly things," he
> thought, and this resolution gave him joy and a kind of
> liberation from the small room.

He wants to show how carnal love may be more than itself, how it
is properly seen as an expression of divine love, as in the erotic
symbolism of the Song of Songs. But the girls themselves are quite
incapable of seeing their lives from this transcendent perspective,
and Father Dowling is going mad.

What good has he done? In this world, none. Society, the
Church, the wretched life of the girls — all go on as before. Isn't it
likely, too, that the Bishop, a master of cynical expediency, may
do more practical good in a time of Depression with his organized
charity drive than one idealistic priest who feels a personal love
for two prostitutes? It is true that love must be personal to be real
— and this is one of Callaghan's great themes in all his work — but
no one can love more than a limited number of people at one time
unless he is God. Only God could love all of society's outcasts. Has
Father Dowling gone mad because he wants to play God? Is this the
fate of saints? Are society and its institutions, even the Church,
always hopelessly corrupt and incapable of redemption through
love? Callaghan offers no comfortable answers to these questions.
One is conscious only that Father Dowling's sweetness and ardor
have left a passing impression on the girls, Mr. Robison, and the
Bishop, and that he is left (like Dean Drone in Stephen Leacock's
Sunshine Sketches) in a state of inner joy and peace that he probably cannot communicate:

> There was a peace within him as he watched the calm,
> eternal water swelling darkly against the one faint streak
> of light, the cold night light on the skyline. High in the
> sky three stars were out. His love seemed suddenly to be
> as steadfast as those stars, as wide as the water, and still
> flowing within him like the cold smooth waves still
> rolling on the shore.

The emphasis here on coldness, distance, and space reinforces the
sense of ambivalence about what love is and what it can do that
runs through the novel. Reference to vast spaces is never altogether comforting in a Canadian work.

In *They Shall Inherit the Earth*, his next novel, Callaghan
addresses himself to the lot of people of rather more ordinary pur-
suits than those of priests and prostitutes, and brings his tale to a
somewhat less equivocal resolution. Two characters in this book
have the simple goodness of the individual who has an inner
integrity untouched by the corruption of a commercial society:
Ross Hillquist and Anna Prychoda. Anna is the more important.

Michael Aikenhead, a prodigal son full of guilt, hatred, and bitter-ness, is saved and redeemed by the love of Anna, and Sheila, his sis-ter, is encouraged by her to rediscover a more basic faith in life. Anna is not a saint or a militant like the later Peggy Sanderson, however; she can live in the imperfect world. All the major charac-ters of this novel are brought by suffering and the encounter with goodness to the condition of humility, tolerance of others, and faith in the good simple life untainted by commerce that Callaghan ardently — and here rather too obviously — preaches. It is, in fact, an unusually preachy and sentimental book, even in a country where overtly moralistic novels have often been the rule.

In this novel, it seems, it is possible to live with integrity, inde-pendent of social pressures, and not be destroyed for one's temerity. This is heartening, but Callaghan's insistence on the potential goodness and basic simplicity of everyone in sight can become wearying. Characters are always becoming "eager" or being struck with simple wonder at important moments. Surely this is senti-mental: the problem is precisely that we aren't that simple a species. It is not easy to love and to forgive or to become free of old antagonisms and bitterness. It is *not* easy for people to live together without social forms, conventions, facades, and pretensions. Perhaps Callaghan felt this himself after writing *They Shall Inherit the Earth*; his next novel is anything but hopeful about the possibil-ity of a true Christianity that might transform society.

In *More Joy in Heaven* the parable of the prodigal son is exam-ined more searchingly. Kip Caley, a paroled bank robber, becomes a kind of circus freak to titillate respectable society. He justifies this role to himself by attempting to become a "mediator" between the criminal and the respectable worlds, but discovers that one is only a distorted mirror-image of the other. The "respectable" are shown to be thieves too, chasing wealth and power. Or else, like Judge Ford, they cannot believe in the possibility of redemption. A true salvation for Kip lies in his friendship with a simple priest, Father Butler, and his love for a simple girl, this time called Julie. But these familiar Callaghan characters live on the fringes of society, and are unable in the end to prevent his destruction. Father Butler says to him:

"That's quite an idea. Maybe the prodigal son had a job
going from feast to feast till the end of his days. Maybe
anybody who wanted an excuse to have a feast invited him
out; maybe he had a job at it for the rest of his life. I wonder
what happened to him after the feasting was over."

What happens is that Kip's disillusionment drives him to his
destruction. Those who are fascinated by Kip are fascinated for the
wrong reasons; they want vicarious excitement and moral self-satis-
faction at the same time: just the mixture of licentiousness and
moral complacency that the old Cecil B. DeMille sin-and-salvation
epics offered to the bored and superficially pious masses. Important
men bolster their false self-images by patronizing Kip. Bored women
get a sexual thrill as they imagine his potential for violence.

This potential in itself remains something of an enigma. Kip is
an "innocent," but his innocence is dangerous. One understands
that his size and strength have always been his most effective
means of self-expression. His violence seems at times to be invol-
untary; it is his instinctive way of commanding attention when he
is frustrated. Yet his occasionally bizarre behavior makes one wonder if Judge Ford is not correct in saying that Kip is, whether he
knows it or not, a danger to others, "a soul full of violence." In the
somewhat melodramatic last chapters he seems so emotionally
unstable as to be capable of anything, and he does in fact shoot a
policeman in a last rejection of social order. Perhaps the world is
to blame for driving him to this, but what does Callaghan think? It
is, as in *Such Is My Beloved*, impossible to determine. What we
know is that Kip cannot affirm safety, justice, and order if they
deny the inner freedom he has always instinctively sought — first
in the excitement of bank robbery and later more positively in
Julie's love.

Socially, Kip's fall from favor is made inevitable by his determination to be a mediator (that is, a saint or Christ-figure) who can
interpret the outcasts to the privileged. He believes also that one
may break the law in the service of charity, and that this is part of
his new freedom. He becomes a freebooter moving perilously
between two worlds until their collision, with apparent inevitability, destroys him.

Kip's last confrontation with society brings about Julie's death as well as his own. In this instance the woman "poor in spirit" inherits the earth in the literal sense. It is an implicit and bitter comment on the ordinary hopefulness of Callaghan's previous novel. Here, tragic ambivalence prevails, as it did in *Such Is My Beloved*. Who is right? Who is truly innocent? Should Kip have felt justified in breaking the law in the name of charity? Could society exist without law and order maintained by force? Did Julie and Father Butler "betray" Kip by reporting the proposed robbery in order to try to save him? Kip dies at peace, but is this achievement worth all the havoc he has just caused? Is there joy in heaven about it?

Is Christianity possible? It is as if Callaghan were forced to tell and re-tell, with variations, the story of the Grand Inquisitor from *The Brothers Karamazov*. Towards the end Kip says: "Butler's a saint, see. But what does that mean? He's against the field, he plays it his own way — a guy like him has to be against the field. If they catch up to him, they'll destroy him." Society cannot tolerate saints, but is society perhaps correct? These questionings take us a long way beyond the story of the real bank robber Red Ryan, which inspired the novel.

We are made aware here of the destructive power of "innocence." In *The Loved and the Lost*, written some years later, this theme is given a more complex and overtly symbolic statement. Peggy Sanderson is another would-be mediator (or mediatrix) who cultivates downward mobility, while Jim McAlpine wants, as his name suggests, to climb upward to the social security and power of the mountain. The topography of Montreal is of immediate use to Callaghan here:

> . . . the mountain is on the island in the river, so the river is always there too, and boat whistles echo all night long against the mountain. . . . Those who wanted things to remain as they were liked the mountain. Those who wanted a change preferred the broad flowing river. But no one could forget either of them.

The two worlds of this novel are geographically located. The mountain is the world of respectability, material wealth, and security. The world of the river is, by contrast, a dark underworld of poverty and passion inhabited by black musicians and by Peggy Sanderson, who prefers their company to that of her own people. The mountain is obviously a male and the river a female symbol.

Peggy seems to believe that the way down is the way upward to the true mountain, the one that is suggested by the cross that stands on top of the actual mountain — that is, to the mountain of spiritual vision. But what does this mean in practice? Her behavior results in bad feeling between blacks and whites, bad feeling between blacks and blacks, and eventually in her own brutal rape and murder. Her innocence seems to be fully as dangerous as Kip Caley's. Peggy seeks to bridge two hostile worlds but is rejected by both and destroyed; in death she represents a vision of reconciliation that has not been achieved.

Jim McAlpine, who loves Peggy, foresees her danger but fails to save her when, finally, she places herself in his hands, because for a moment he loses his faith in her innocence. He is likened to Orpheus, and he loses his Eurydice to the world of death as he feared he would:

> In a moment of jealous doubt his faith in her had weakened, he had lost his view of her, and so she had vanished. She had vanished off the earth. And now he was alone.

Orpheus, as we know, lost Eurydice by looking behind for her, not by losing sight of her, but Jim's failure is his failure to keep faith with Peggy's vision. If he cannot truly see her, she must vanish, for no one else from either world can believe in her.

The story of Orpheus and Eurydice is classical. It has no immediate Christian resonances. But Peggy is also likened to Shaw's Saint Joan, that is, to a militant whom society makes a martyr:

> . . . she, like Joan, lived and acted by her own secret intuitions. Joan had shattered her world, and Peggy shattered people too. . . . She would shatter all the people who lived on the mountain and the people who prayed on the mountain.

Joan had to die, he thought with a sharp pang, simply because she was what she was.

Peggy may be invulnerable in the spiritual sphere but she cannot, it seems, live on the earth, for everyone fails her:

> As the sun touched the top of the mountain and suddenly brightened the snow, McAlpine stopped, watching it intently. He had a swift wild fancy: the streets on the slopes of the mountain were echoing to the pounding of horses' hoofs. All the proud men on their white horses came storming down the slope of the mountain in a ruthless cavalry charge, the white horses whirling and snorting in the snow. And Peggy was on foot in the snow. She didn't own a white horse. She didn't want to. She didn't care. And he was beside her; but he drew back out of the way of the terrifying hoofs and they rode over her. And now he was left alone on the street, and the young women who knew his story were staring at him sorrowfully, all saying the same thing.
> Then he heard a voice saying, "What do you care what they say?"

The white horses represent everyone else's psychological insecurities and their need for respectability; Peggy possesses her own soul, she doesn't need a white horse, and this constitutes a threat to them. Striving up the mountain of material success, these people are really, as the vision indicates, moving downward on the spiritual plane. They are on a collision course, it seems, with the saint.

It is a moving and beautiful climax to the story, but can we accept Peggy as a saint and leave it at that? Doesn't she, like Father Dowling and Kip Caley, do rather more harm than good to herself and others? She is fascinated by two symbolic objects that seem to "go together," the statue of a leopard about to spring and an antique church — presumably because she seeks the transformation of biological energy into spiritual energy — but does she know what she is about? Her attachment to black people is the result of an intense childhood involvement with a black family whose warmth and affection had made up for the emotional inadequacy of her own family life. But she is no longer a child; she is an attractive woman, and it is inevitable that her black friends will think that her interest is sexual. In her "innocence" of this aspect of the world's ways Peggy does not realize that she is the inevitable catalyst for jealousy and hatred. Like Father Dowling, she could be regarded (from the perspective of this world) as a clinical case — someone who has refused to grow up and face reality.

Callaghan seems concerned that we accept that Peggy's friendships with black men are not consciously sexual, but, as a female student of mine put it to me one day, what difference would it make if she had slept with every black man in Montreal? Her vision of brotherhood between the races is neither more nor less valid because she is or is not 'chaste', to use a quaint old term. Nor is the vision invalidated if we choose to regard her simply as a fool. So I guess we are left with the usual ambivalence: she is a fool or a saint, or both. She does harm, unwittingly, to everyone she meets but she leaves Jim McAlpine with a sense of her values. Her words, "What do you care what they say?", echo in his mind as a reproach to pretentious, materialistic, ungenerous, and hypocritical Canadian society. Indeed, the sentiment behind the words may be felt in a great deal of Canadian fiction. Mrs. Bentley in *As For Me and My House* and the dying Hagar Shipley in *The Stone Angel* could make these words their joint epitaph: "What do you care what they say?"

Perhaps Canadian "saints" have distinctive characteristics. Let's be anachronistic for a moment — looking at Canadian literature as one evolving organism — and consider Leonard Cohen's definition of the "saint" in *Beautiful Losers*:

> A saint is someone who has achieved a remote human possibility. It is impossible to say what that possibility is. I think it has something to do with the energy of love. Contact with this energy results in the exercise of a kind of balance in the chaos of existence. A saint does not dissolve the chaos; if he did the world would have changed long ago. I do not think that a saint dissolves the chaos even for himself, for there is something arrogant and warlike in the notion of a man setting the universe in order. It is a kind of

balance that is his glory. He rides the drifts like an escaped
ski. His course is a caress of the hill. His track is a drawing
of the snow in a moment of its particular arrangement with
wind and rock. Something in him so loves the world that he
gives himself to the laws of gravity and chance. Far from
flying with the angels, he traces with the fidelity of a
seismograph needle the state of the solid bloody landscape.
His house is dangerous and finite, but he is at home in the
world. He can love the shapes of human beings, the fine and
twisted shapes of the heart. It is good to have among us such
men, such balancing monsters to love.

The first three sentences of this passage are vague enough to apply
to a sword-swallower. But the rest is very illuminating, if one
thinks of Peggy Sanderson, who expresses "a kind of balance" (the
balance between leopard and church, between the beauty of terror
and the beauty of peace, to borrow a phrase from Duncan Campbell
Scott) and a love for the world in which she feels at home (even if
the world does not feel at home with her), but who is unable to dis-
solve the world's chaos even for herself. Cohen does not say the
saint will be destroyed for his achievement, but most of his own
characters, his beautiful losers, do suffer this fate in one form or
another. Nor does he speak of fool-saints, but Robertson Davies
notes in *Fifth Business* that this is a Jewish notion. Father Dowling,
Cohen's F., and Davies' Mrs. Dempster possess an ambivalent
"virtue tainted with madness," as Davies phrases it in *Fifth
Business*; all come up against the coldness, the lack of generosity or
imagination in Canadian middle-class values. No doubt the concept
of the fool-saint is Jewish (that is, universal), but it seems to have
flourished in philistine Canada; I doubt that Cohen was influenced
by Callaghan, or Davies by *Beautiful Losers*, and I would guess that
Callaghan was influenced by Dostoievsky — in this regard by *The
Idiot* — but the fool-saint has been at home in Canada a number of
times. Dean Drone and Adele Wiseman's Hoda in *Crackpot* may be
other examples. It is arguable that he or she belongs — as an idea —
to all times and places; but surely some countries, especially cold
northern ones, may need his or her disturbing presence more than
others. It's possible that as Canadians grow less narrow, philistine,

and colonial-minded, we will have less and less need of the fool-saint. His or her message will have been assimilated (to whatever degree is possible) by the ordinary, relatively unbalanced, unmonstrous rest of us.

Callaghan himself leaves the "saints" behind in his next novel, *The Many-Coloured Coat.* It is his least successful work. The major difficulty is Harry Lane, the central character; he is unattractive both in his palmy days of success and glad-handing and in his bitterly vindictive drive for vindication, and this makes it difficult for the reader to care very much about what happens to him. Therefore, there is no real drama. Harry doesn't seem at any point to be a very nice (or an interestingly bad) man. Again, the story is not very credible; why would anybody care about his antics after a week or so? Callaghan is always somewhat given to the arbitrary manipulation of plot and situation, but here it is much more noticeable than usual. Still, we are on familiar ground, and the novel is at least interesting as a further exploration of Callaghan's obsession. Harry Lane, who is by no stretch of anyone's imagination a "saint" or genuine mediator, is, however, an "innocent," and he demonstrates that "innocence" can be a vice, if not a malignant illusion. In this novel Callaghan exhausts this problem (or fascinating pseudo-problem) and is thus able to remark (through the person of Sam) in *A Passion in Rome*: "I haven't the slightest interest in innocence. Furthermore, you're intelligent enough, I hope, to know that the whole human race hasn't had any innocence for about twenty-five thousand years." Just so. Innocence, in Dean Drone, Father Dowling, or Peggy Sanderson, involves a degree of ignorance of self and the world.

A Passion in Rome had a bad reception, for the most part, from public and reviewers. Callaghan has confessed to being upset by this, and he had every right to be upset, for this is in fact his finest novel and a major achievement by any standard.

Where (if we forget for a moment the author's creative genius that wove all the elements together) did this astonishing book come from? From an acquaintance with Rome, obviously; it is interesting to note that the removal (on paper) from good, gray Toronto, as it then was, to the simultaneously real and fabulous cities of Montreal and Rome helped Callaghan to grow as an artist.

Perhaps from certain brief glimpses of Zelda Fitzgerald's behavior remembered decades later, as a comparison of one or two scenes from the novel with the corresponding ones in *That Summer in Paris* indicates. Did Callaghan's admiration for *Tender is the Night* stimulate his interest in the man and woman who could avoid the disaster of Nicole and Dick Diver, of Zelda and Scott Fitzgerald? Did the novel grow from the small story of the broken-down singer who makes a comeback in *The Many-Coloured Coat*? From what was then known of the character and fate of Marilyn Monroe? Or of Edith Piaf? From memories of Daisy Miller? Certainly it is a story of our time and also, as Callaghan makes more complex use of Rome — that many-layered, more complex city — than he did of Montreal, a story of all times, of our psychic history, our infinitely slow but perceptible progress from savage and mysterious beginnings which are, however, themselves the source of our spiritual energies. His Anna Connel comes to embody both the savagery and the Christian message of Rome.

The novel adds a new twist to what one might call Callaghan's "fable"; perhaps it dissolves the fable altogether (though it reappears in a more mature form in later work). Anna (or Carla) is at the opposite pole from the person who possesses that inner integrity found in such previous characters as Anna Prychoda, Father Butler, Peggy Sanderson, or the refined gold-hearted whore Annie Laurie, who figures in *The Many-Coloured Coat*. Carla is an extreme case of the person who doesn't possess her own soul, who lacks any degree of serenity or self-possession. This extreme is obviously as potentially dangerous as the other, but Sam Raymond, Callaghan's hero, manages the difficult trick of restoring her to herself (or, to put it another way, of assisting at her creation as a whole person) without destroying himself. She must ultimately leave him, as a mental patient must become independent of her psychiatrist, and he must suffer because he loves her and has even been tempted to make her dependent forever, but he achieves nevertheless a sense of spiritual triumph, accepting, as she does, the necessity of her departure.

It is a moving story extremely well told. Carla is the most interesting and the most credible woman in all of Callaghan's work. His editorializing tendencies are for once perfectly integrated into the narrative flow. There is a deftness of touch, a rightness of tone, incident, and characterization, a genuine sense of inevitability that are lacking in the earlier novels. From Carla's first mysterious appearance on a dark street, through her partly escapist and partly therapeutic identification with historic Rome (with an unforgettable and chilling scene in which she feeds chunks of meat to the cats in the Colosseum), to her eventual return to her own time and place, one is held fascinated as a spiritual process, a sacred mystery, unfolds. The death of the old pope and the election of the new provide an appropriate literal and symbolic background for Carla's and Sam's death and resurrection as more whole human beings. For he too is transformed by the encounter. A lonely failed painter in a mid-life crisis, he comes to terms with himself in his attempt to be a Pygmalion in life.

Callaghan's more recent novels, *A Fine and Private Place* and *Close to the Sun Again*, share with his earlier work a profound sense of moral and spiritual ambiguity and complexity. *A Fine and Private Place* seems, at first, to be a neglected writer's complaint, a somewhat embarrassing *roman à clef* populated by pale spectres of Callaghan himself, his chief critical defender Edmund Wilson, and a much-maligned Northrop Frye. But more interesting things are going on as well. There is, as usual in Callaghan, an emphasis on the ultimate mystery of things and human beings as they are, and of both life and art — what can't be explained, analyzed, or categorized in terms of the theory of Northrop Frye or anyone else (including, presumably, Jacques Maritain). There is sharp observation of Toronto in the 1970s, and a well-handled account of the difficult relationship of young lovers. The girl Lisa discovers her complicity with the forces of irrationality and darkness in the course of a tale in which it is Eugene Shore himself — the distinguished novelist whose books, as described, closely resemble *More Joy in Heaven, Such Is My Beloved,* and *The Loved and the Lost* — who falls victim to the social and psychological insecurity as well as the exhilaration of murder in others — as Kip Caley and Peggy Sanderson did before him. In this process no-one's motives seem to be pure or readily explicable: tragic ambivalence prevails again.

Of special interest, of course, is the account of Shore's work that is developed by Al Delaney, a young scholar who abandons Norman

Mailer in order to devote himself to his fellow Torontonian. Shore is seen as a kind of anarchist who hates "cops" or rigidly defined authority of any kind. His characters are clown-criminals or "clown-outlaws in the circus of life." Is this another way of saying fool-saint? These individuals are (like Lisa and perhaps even the murderous cop in this book) "like lovers knowing only the law of their own love." Tragic heroes possessed of extraordinary daring, they enlarge the sense of life in those who observe them. Shore holds such people in the light of his love, we are told. All of this — if it is meant seriously — suggests to me that Callaghan might not altogether go along with my own view of his work (since I don't see him as being wholly on the side of Dowling, Caley, Sanderson, and Co. even if he does "love" them) but I am unrepentant. After all, he has not himself suffered the fate of Eugene Shore; he continues to live with the world as it is. And more may have been going on in him during his periods of greatest creativity than his late, conscious reflections can indicate. I still think "ambivalence" is the operative word, except perhaps in the case of *A Passion in Rome* with its positive resolution in spiritual rebirth.

Close to the Sun Again is a simpler fable in which a hollow man — a distinguished naval commander and corporation executive who becomes a police commissioner (a sure sign of sterility and living death for Eugene Shore) — is able before he dies to relive those events of the Second World War that brought him close to human passion in all its ambivalence and power for the only time in his life. He had suppressed this experience until the last. The psychology adumbrated here may be a bit simplistic or implausible, as it often is in Callaghan's books, but the power of the flashback scenes of men at sea is remarkable. The excursion to sea is an interesting departure from the author's usual urban world.

An even more remarkable departure takes Callaghan to ancient Jerusalem in *A Time for Judas*, one of his best novels. Here the chief "clown-outlaws" are Simon, one of the thieves crucified with Jesus, and Jesus himself. These are the men whose inner freedom, that kingdom of heaven within, society cannot tolerate. Others who partake of this mystery are Judas, who "betrays" Jesus only to take his part in the "story" that may inspire the future transformation of humanity; Mary Magdalene, who is apparently the lover of

Jesus (for Callaghan, like Father Dowling, here departs from his
Church in seeing sexuality as a central vehicle for divine love);
Pontius Pilate, who secretly sympathizes with Jesus; and Philo, the
author's Greek narrator. In this book the nature of Callaghan's
Christianity is at last made quite clear: it is chiefly a matter of
exalting that secret inner world of love and wonder that so often in
his books comes tragically into conflict with the more usual mores
of the modern urban world. As it was in ancient Jerusalem or
Rome, he seems to say, so it is in modern Montreal or Toronto.

A further novel of interest, *Our Lady of the Snows*, expanded
from the long story "The Enchanted Pimp," adds little to
Callaghan's "myth"; but it displays his faults, virtues, and continuing preoccupations quite as one might expect. It is populated by a
number of stock characters or puppets, most of them not so well
realized as their atmospheric Toronto setting. Ilona Tomory, the
Callaghan ideal woman, successor to Peggy Sanderson and others
(but now allowed survival and even a happy ending), is the daughter of an aristocratic Hungarian-refugee couple down on their luck
but keeping up a certain style — symbolized by an impressive-
looking but repeatedly taped mink coat that has seen better days.
Beautiful and mysterious, Ilona becomes a hooker who services
only unhappy (though not vicious) men in need of her compassion
and the "illusion of intimacy" she creates.

Such a "sister of mercy" is credible, I think, but her ministrations
are more usually free of monetary charge (as Leonard Cohen would
perhaps attest); however, Ilona is not a "hooker-healer" for very long
in any case before she devotes herself to a single (conveniently rich)
young man, who takes her to Mexico but loses her because he
doesn't yet grasp that she is more precious than the mystical will-o'-
the-wisps he is pursuing. She is last seen (or heard of) married most
happily to a wise and earthy Greek freighter-captain who appreciates
her qualities and even admires her for her past. They live on board:
"Ilona was at home on the sea, at one with the waters, the nurturing
waters washing around all human shores, Ilona with her ancient gift,
sailing the seas of God." Every retired hooker should be so lucky; a
kind of compendium of Mary Magdalene, Midge, Julie, Peggy, Annie
Laurie, and perhaps others, Ilona is a beautiful, loving woman with
whom many sensible men might want to spend their lives.

Moreover, her career as a prostitute is brief enough that she does not ever seem to be seriously promiscuous. She just has to find the right man, that's all. This makes the latest treatment of Callaghan's sexual-religious myth a good deal less subversive in its implications than *Such Is My Beloved* or *The Loved and the Lost* (not to mention, once again, *Beautiful Losers*). But *Our Lady of the Snows*, neither the best nor the worst of the old master's works, is nevertheless a reasonably engrossing tale, mainly because the central character is finally not Ilona herself but the pimp and enforcer Edmund J. Dubuque, a somewhat more interesting personage because of his quite convincing mixture of good and evil qualities ("innocence" has been left far behind by now) and because of the blurred urban borderline between legitimate and criminal business that he straddles.

As always, Callaghan is stronger dealing with the urban setting than with character. But Jay is one of his more effective creations. His fatal limitation is his cynicism. His opposite, the bartender and would-be writer Gil (unfortunately a puppet with almost no semblance of fictional life), avers (as Leonard Cohen does): "There's as much mystery in dirt and dung as there is in heaven." That's "what they say at the top of the mountain." This is all very familiar by now. But it is interesting, observing this pair of commentators who are making Ilona's story, to speculate that Callaghan himself is part shrewd observer (Dubuque) and part sentimental romantic (Gil); he has split himself here between his two interpreters of Ilona (that is, of life's passion and mystery). The demands of the material realm and those of the spiritual are thus separated again — to indicate that inner division that generates all of the author's work? — even if Ilona has triumphantly reunited them; or perhaps she has transcended the duality altogether in removing herself from her first world. Having discarded her mink-coat of pretension, she sails the wide mythic seas of God. She has left the city altogether though her legend lingers there. Her creator, however, stays put.

For Callaghan, in most of his work, explores the life of the spirit as it is manifested in the modern city. He remains a religious novelist in naturalistic garb. (This seems to be the right word, despite his reiterated insistence that he is not in the millinery business — that is, not concerned with fashion — because of the significance attached to clothing in some of the novels.) He continues to explore human moral and spiritual ambivalence. Still, in *A Time for Judas*, as in *A Passion in Rome*, his best book, he seems to have, to some degree, resolved the tension between two conceptions of reality that was so striking a feature of his earlier parables. Flesh and spirit, time and eternity here cooperate in the work of redemption.

I have said nothing about Callaghan's short stories. They have been praised, and rightly praised, for decades. But it is his novels, whatever their flaws, that best reflect the Canadian tensions as they are felt in his distinctive urban world, which is essentially a man's world of bars, racetracks, downtown, boxing, reporters, prostitutes, bookies, petty criminals, and some priests. It is a world of identifiable modern cities, four of them (if we throw in Paris), but also an inner psychic world, a world in turmoil, struggling to reconcile, or at least hold in meaningful balance within itself, the perspectives of Hemingway, Freud, Marx, Dostoievsky, and Maritain (among others). This can, of course, be the source of formal strain. But if the novelist is sometimes guilty of manipulating his material in rather too obvious and arbitrary ways, he has also impressive strengths even in the weakest of the novels. One thinks of the beautiful economy of words that can convey so much in *Such Is My Beloved* and *More Joy in Heaven*, of the impressive social panorama of *The Loved and The Lost* and of ancient Jerusalem in *A Time for Judas*, of the sureness and perfect integrity of *A Passion in Rome*; even *They Shall Inherit the Earth* and *The Many-Coloured Coat*, the novels that are least convincing, repay one's attention, since they explore important themes. Indeed, Morley Callaghan is one of our most important novelists; he has earned a lasting place in "Canadian" literature, and furthered its development, whether he intended that or not.

4 Third Solitude:
Mordecai Richler's Jewish Canadians

Vel, anyway, all I can say, is Tanks Gods, for Mordecai
Richler. He is a bad Jew and a worse Canadian but he
tells it as it is.
— Larry Zolf

What I am looking for are the values with which in
this time a man can live with honour.
— Mordecai Richler

Mordecai Richler has, it seems, been both embarrassed and obsessed
by his identity as Jew and Canadian. Though he offers little solid
evidence of knowing much about Canada beyond a few streets in
Montreal, he remains very Canadian. Feeling a strong (and natural)
affinity with American Jewish writers of his own generation, he
nevertheless chose — after his time in Paris — to live in London,
England, and not in New York. A man originally of the left, he
expresses great admiration for the very English and very right-wing
satirical genius of Evelyn Waugh. Surely rather a Canadian balance
of perspectives. Inevitably, it seems, he has come home again,
though it was apparently quite unthinkable in the 1950s for him to
do what Morley Callaghan and Hugh MacLennan had already
done: live and work in Canada.

The Apprenticeship of Duddy Kravitz, its companion piece and complement *St. Urbain's Horseman*, as well as their later successors *Joshua Then and Now* and *Solomon Gursky Was Here*, express in their own ways a return to Richler's roots in Jewish Montreal, to the third solitude of that city. We are back in A.M. Klein's ghetto, at Fletcher's Field High School, to be exact, where uncomprehending WASP teachers do battle with Jewish urchins. The model for this school, Baron Byng, graduated Klein and Irving Layton (not to mention Klein's close friend David Lewis) some years before it graduated Mordecai Richler. No doubt it deserves a species of immortality.

One reads *Duddy Kravitz*, easily the funniest Canadian work of fiction since Leacock's *Sunshine Sketches*, with increasing delight and, at least initially, a certain degree of bemusement. It is picaresque, it has grotesquely eccentric characters and marvelous comic dialogue, it concerns a very young man of extraordinary drive and enterprise coming to — what? Not maturity, surely. What, finally, is it all about? Love? Money? Survival? Tribe and family? Land?

Love or friendship that extend beyond his immediate family, his own tribe, are luxuries Duddy cannot comprehend even while he has them:

> "I suppose," Mr. Calder said, pushing his plate away, "that I should have expected something like this from you. I had hoped we were friends."
>
> "Sure we are," Duddy had replied, flushing. "But friends help each other."
>
> . . . . .
>
> White men, Duddy thought. *Ver gerharget*. With them you just didn't make deals. You had to diddle. They were like those girls you had to discuss God or the Book-of-the-Month with so all the time they could pretend not to know you had a hand up their skirt, but just try to take it away. Just try, buster. He's offended, Duddy thought, but he made the deal all the same. Two-fifty more a ton, sure. I suppose he wanted

me to play golf with him for eighteen years first or something. I haven't got that much time to waste, he thought.

. . . . .

"What do you want from me, Mr. Calder?"
"I enjoy your company."
"Come off it. I amuse you. That's what you mean."
"You're a friend of mine. I take a fatherly interest in you."
"Yeah," Duddy said, "then how come you never introduce me to any of your other friends?"
"They might not understand you."
"You mean I might try to make a deal with them like I did with you over the crap and that would embarrass you. I'm a little Jewish pusherke. Right?"
"You're acting like a young man on the verge of a nervous breakdown."

Whose side is Richler on in such cross-cultural exchanges as this? At first, one is inclined to say: Duddy's, of course. Calder has cultivated and patronized him for his entertainment value. But, on reflection, one realizes that Hugh Thomas Calder, the bored WASP businessman, has a case too. No doubt Duddy amuses him, but Calder also admires (and perhaps envies) Duddy's spirit, his potential for accomplishment. There is no reason to doubt Calder's concern for Duddy's welfare, especially when his diagnosis is so accurate. Probably these two individuals of different class and religious background are incapable of understanding one another, or the forces that have shaped the other, very fully, but human sympathy is offered to Duddy, and he is unable to accept it. Like Stephen Leacock, like T.C. Haliburton, like Susanna Moodie for that matter, Richler explores the comedy of cultural tensions when he involves Duddy with an eccentric WASP businessman, a loving and honest French-Canadian girl, and an innocent, worshipful American friend. But Duddy fails every such test, from the initial encounter with the ineffectual liberal teacher MacPherson, on: he remains incapable of the transcendence of cultural barriers suggested by Klein in *The Rocking Chair*. He is fiercely and admirably loyal only to his own family.

Motherless, Duddy does not understand women or realize until
he is driven to a kind of breakdown in her absence that he needs
and loves Yvette without wanting to. The nature of their relationship is indicated in small exchanges such as these:

> Yvette wanted to wait, but Duddy insisted, and they made
> love on the carpet.
> "I don't get it," Duddy said. "Imagine guys getting married
> and tying themselves down to one single broad for a whole
> lifetime when there's just so much stuff around."
> "People fall in love," Yvette said. "It happens."
> "Planes crash too," Duddy said. "Listen, I've got an
> important letter to write. We'll eat soon. OK?"
> She didn't answer and Duddy began to type.

Duddy begins to realize his need for Yvette but eventually loses
her because of the ruthlessness of his drive for property.

Money is the most important thing in Duddy's world, and it is
easy for him to misunderstand his grandfather's saying that a man
without land is a nobody. The old man of two ghettoes, one in the
old and one in the new world, dreams ineffectually of a pastoral
world, perhaps (as in Klein's Zionist poems) of Israel. Duddy
dreams instead of development and exploitation and a vulgar but
lucrative resort. The new world with which he must contend is
the world of Jerry Dingleman, the Boy Wonder, and of Mr. Cohen:

> "Listen here, my young Mr. Kravitz, you want to be a
> saint? Go to Israel and plant oranges on a *kibbutz*. I'll give
> you the fare with pleasure. Only I know you and I know two
> weeks after you landed you'd be scheming to corner the
> schmaltz herring market or something. We're two of a kind,
> you know. Listen, listen here. My attitude even to my oldest
> and dearest customer is this," he said, making a throat-
> cutting gesture. "If I thought he'd be good for half a cent
> more a ton I'd squeeze it out of him. A plague on all the
> *goyim*, that's my motto. The more money I make the better
> care I take of my own, the more I'm able to contribute to our

hospital, the building of Israel, and other worthy causes. So a *goy* is crippled and you think you're to blame. Given the chance he would have crippled you," he shouted, "or thrown you into a furnace like six million others. You think I didn't lose relatives? I lost relatives."

Cohen, as Richler tells us, exaggerates his own ruthlessness and crookedness, yet he does seem to have been guilty of criminal negligence and of receiving stolen goods in his struggle to achieve material security for himself and his family. Like most of Richler's characters, he is far from being unsympathetic; indeed, he is rather likeable. Richler's understanding and compassion are extended to the Cohens and Harry Steins and Duddys and Virgils and Calders and MacPhersons of this world at the same time as they are satirized. This is the mixture of frailties that makes the human animal.

It is Richler's shifting perspective, his *concerned* and compassionate criticism, that places him next to Leacock or Klein (even if he had never read them), and separates him forever from Evelyn Waugh, however much he may admire him. *The Incomparable Atuk*, Richler's first attempt to function as a kind of Canadian Waugh by manipulating Canadian caricatures and stereotypes in absurd situations, is funny and even instructive without ever being very memorable or profound. The later *Cocksure* is somewhat more successful in this vein, but neither book has the compassion and depth of *Duddy Kravitz* or *St. Urbain's Horseman*, let alone the savage Swiftian vision of Waugh. Richler is much kinder. His ambivalence, his irony, his ability to hold a number of perspectives and attitudes in tension — these are Canadian.

I sometimes think (oversimplifying, to make a point) that there are two kinds of Canadians, though I've only been describing one of them. First, there are the fanatics, of whom we've always had heaps — all those fierce nineteenth-century Protestants and Catholics who wanted to continue the religious wars in the New World. Their twentieth-century spiritual descendants cling to one narrow rectitude, creed, region, language, patriotism or another (and one could include here those artists who cling to rigid aesthetic theories). Second, there are those whose consciousness transcends cultural barriers, those who seek compromise or synthesis, communication, understanding, mutual respect — in a word — community: the crafty Macdonalds and Lauriers and Kings and Pearsons who have held the country together; the artists, such as Klein and Richler and Laurence and Purdy, who also see that Canada is a coalition of minorities and regions that must, frequently, agree to disagree.

But it is inevitable that a writer like Richler, who depicts the faults as well as the virtues of his own immediate group, will be misunderstood and called anti-Semitic by those whose sympathies, like those of Duddy Kravitz, have narrow boundaries. All too often — in Scots, French, Jews, Indians, or whatever — charity begins at home, and stays there. And, understandably, the Montreal Jewish community that endured subtle and not-so-subtle forms of anti-Semitism in earlier decades is very touchy about its public image, about providing ammunition to the potential enemy. But this is to miss the point in Richler's case; he is on record as saying that the working class Jew has more in common with the working-class Gentile than with the bosses of either persuasion, and his satirical account of rich, vulgar Jews is not primarily concerned with their Jewishness, nor is it without an element of affection.

Richler is a satirist and a moralist, a type of the Canadian small "c" conservative (consider Jake Hersh's reverence for "the late great Reb Shmul Johnson" in *St. Urbain's Horseman*). Both he and persons close to him have suggested that in another age he might well have been a rabbi. Duddy's Uncle Benjy, like the younger Richler a socialist and moralist, perhaps speaks for him when he says:

> "There used to be . . . some dignity in being against the synagogue. With a severe orthodox rabbi there were things to quarrel about. There was some pleasure. But this cream-puff of a synagogue, this religious drugstore, you might as well spend your life being against the *Reader's Digest*. They've taken all the mystery out of religion."

The complexity and apparent absurdity of the modern world encourages in Richler a vein of near-nihilistic parody: *Cocksure* is the most extravagant expression of it. But here we have Virgil's epileptic's newsletter, a devastating send-up of the over-sensitivity of minority groups, and the hilarious "avant garde" Bar Mitzvah film (even funnier, of course, in the film of the novel, and the only respect in which the film improves on the novel). Then there is this sort of black comedy:

> "You see," Virgil said, "it was a blessing in disguise. I'm glad you're not angry though. I mean well, remember I said you'd be remembered as the Branch Rickey like of the Health Handicappers? Well, what if Jackie Robinson had turned out to be a two hundred hitter? That's what I turned out to be, you know. A prize flop. But if not for the accident there'd be no *Crusader*. It might have taken me years and years to get going. See my point?"
> "Sure, Virgie. Sure thing."
> There was a kind of flask attachment under the mattress of Virgil's bed and it was gradually filling with urine.

All of this is meant to demonstrate an absurdist maxim (again enunciated by Uncle Benjy, in his very important farewell letter to Duddy): "Experience doesn't teach: it deforms." This saying — which seems to be borne out by the development, physical and/or moral, of Dingleman, Aunt Ida, Virgil, and Duddy himself — would be cause for despair, were it not for the balancing insistence on free will and freedom of moral choice that comes later in the letter.

This brings us to two central and related questions about the novel. Is it genuinely "realistic" or "naturalistic," or is it a fantastic parade of grotesques, a satiric fantasia aspiring to the condition of *Cocksure*? Is it inexorably determined by brutal circumstances that Duddy become a bastard, as monstrous as the monstrous Boy Wonder himself, or can he choose to be something else? It seems to me that ambivalence is once again the key word. Richler raises questions that he will not answer.

Consider the manipulation of time in the novel. In the early chapters we get the story of Duddy and Mr. MacPherson, the well-meaning but ineffectual teacher, a fussy WASP, a frustrated liberal turned drinker, whose invalid wife collapses and dies after an obscene phone-call from Duddy. Duddy does not come off very well in this, and we are reminded of the MacPherson episode, perhaps

Duddy's first atrocity, at key points thereafter, including the novel's penultimate page. But after this initial episode we are provided with the extenuating circumstances of Duddy's family and background, and then with the story of his mistreatment at the resort. These inspire considerable sympathy: nothing is simple or clear-cut.

"Where Duddy Kravitz sprung from the boys grew up dirty and sad, spiky also, like grass beside the railroad tracks." This and what follows beautifully enlists our sympathy for Duddy, who has no mother, whose father is a highly likeable but not very bright cab-driver and pimp, and whose favored brother is a moral weakling. He is loved well only by his pathetic old grandfather. He has, we recall, invented an extra brother as a means of coping with his emotional deprivation. He is highly nervous, inwardly desperate, driven. It is understandable that he becomes a gang leader among his friends. It is a world where one has to fight for survival, and Duddy is determined to be somebody, like the Boy Wonder, at any rate not a loser.

But the enthusiasm for Duddy's energy and ruthlessness evinced by such critics as Warren Tallman is misguided in an "American" direction because it tells only half of the story and distorts the shape of the novel: Richler's intentions, as I've suggested, seem to have been more complex.

MacPherson was, to a large extent, responsible for his own tragedy. But Duddy's treatment of Yvette and Virgil is a good deal nearer to being wholly reprehensible. He is indirectly responsible for Virgil's paralysis and cannot resist the temptation to swindle him in order to complete his purchase of land. In so doing, he loses the love of Yvette, Virgil, and his grandfather; he is left only with the stupid admiration of Max and the sadistic satisfaction of having chased the physically and morally deformed Dingleman off his land. He chooses Dingleman as his enemy, a choice one might applaud, were it not so obvious that he is becoming more and more like him. His gesture is therefore an evasion; he has become his own worst enemy.

"Experience doesn't teach: it deforms." Is this then the book's lesson? Benjy also writes:

There's more to you than mere money-lust, Duddy, but I'm

afraid for you. You're two people, that's why. The scheming little bastard I saw so easily and the fine, intelligent boy underneath that your grandfather, bless him, saw. But you're coming of age soon and you'll have to choose. A boy can be two, three, four potential people, but a man is only one. He murders the others.

According to this notion, Duddy had (and perhaps still has) the potential to be more than another Boy Wonder or Sammy Glick. Richler leaves us with a balance of philosophies. He doesn't come out unequivocally for either the determination of environmental pressures or the freedom of moral choice. He only suggests each possibility as it occurs in the confused mind of the dying Benjy. He refuses, ultimately, to judge Duddy (as Morley Callaghan refused to judge his characters, as Leacock refused to judge) since he cannot know whether Duddy has a choice or not. We have here neither a naturalistic novel nor a satiric fantasy, but something in-between: a realistic account with significant distortions, another Canadian hybrid. It is a marvelous book.

Jake Hersh, the hero of *St. Urbain's Horseman*, helps to reveal Richler's most important concern: "the values with which in this time a man can live with honour." When he meets Duddy, after several years, in the earlier book, he is honest in his reaction to him:

> Duddy grinned. "Hoo-haw," he said, and he poured Hersh another drink. "It's so good to see you. We ought to have reunions like. When I think of all the swell characters I used to know at FFHS. Hey, remember the time that lush-head MacPherson accused me of killing his wife?"
> "He's in an asylum."
> "Wha'?"
> "He's in Verdun."
> "That's show biz, I guess," Duddy said, flushing.
> "I think I'd better be off. Thanks for the drink."
> "Aw, come on. Sit down."
> "Why pretend we're friends, Duddy? We hated each other at school."

Interestingly enough, the two do become friends. Hersh, like
Richler himself, can see the good as well as the bad in Duddy. He
is a kind of artist, a man struggling for moral vision — thus he is
obviously much closer to his creator than most of Richler's other
significant characters.

Hersh has a fantasy hero, an alter ego, in his mysterious cousin
Joey, the Horseman of St. Urbain Street who (Hersh believes) tracks
down Nazi war-criminals. Like Klein's Uncle Melech in *The
Second Scroll*, the Horseman represents the heroic spirit of Jewry in
a time of great moral confusion. But Jake, unlike Klein's narrator,
has two alter egos: the other is Harry Stein who involves him in a
sordid sex scandal. Jake becomes fascinated by the squalid Harry, a
"little man" eaten up by spite and envy, one of Richler's most successful comic creations. If the Horseman is meant to be heroic,
Harry is decidedly anti-heroic: they are the poles of Jake's possible
self, and perhaps of the Jewish response to the terror of modern history.

Ironically, it seems likely as well that the real Joey is not much
better than a common thug, but Jake clings to his heroic fantasy as
a remedy for his recurrent nightmares about Dr. Joseph Mengele
and for his middle-aged obsession with, and disgust at, the ultimate facts of physical decline and death. *St. Urbain's Horseman* is
an ambitious and impressive novel, funny, sad, and powerful by
turns, even if it lacks something of the exuberant freshness of
Duddy Kravitz.

Much the same can be said of *Joshua Then and Now*, a less
powerful but structurally more complex and sophisticated treatment of the major themes of its predecessor. This novel has a variety of interesting Canadian and international settings and a large
cast of comic characters with wonderfully funny things to say.
Indeed, it is the novel as film-script (though the subsequent film is
much less complex). Intricately plotted, it is a weaving together of
the disparate times and places and impressions that make a life, a
consciousness. It is worth noting here that *The Watch That Ends
the Night*, *The Stone Angel*, and *The Diviners* are other (and earlier) notable Canadian novels of "then and now," replete with flashbacks, but they are structurally much simpler. In his deep ambivalence about the mysteries of time and experience Richler is here

more the comic successor to Callaghan than to the national chron-
icler MacLennan; Margaret Laurence is MacLennan's more obvious heir in terms of Protestant religious sensibility, emotional
power, and concern for the shape of Canadian history.

One must immediately add to this, however, that *Solomon
Gursky Was Here*, which belatedly enlarges the scope of Richler's
imaginative universe, provides his own distinctive and characteris-
tically sardonic version of that history. The Franklin expedition,
the Bronfman saga, and even Montreal-Jewish literary history are
reinterpreted, even reinvented in often hilarious ways. A synthetic
parody of Canadian mythic identity is developed in terms of a
blend of Judaism, the mystic North, and the west coast aboriginal
stories of the trickster, Raven. Perhaps most interesting, at least
when one is considering his own career, is the implication that
Richler is here acknowledging that, in the guise of his chief protagonist Moses Berger, he is the uneasy literary son of a compromised
A.M. Klein — that is, the poet L.B. Berger, who is corrupted by his
association with the Gurskys. ("Kleinberger" was one of Klein's
poetic alter egos, let it be noted, and "L." and "B." are adjacent to
"M." and "A.," respectively, in the alphabet.)

At this point, one is inclined to ask: why have so many of
Canada's best and most significant writers in English been Jews?
One thinks, for instance, of Klein, Layton, Cohen, Richler, Adele
Wiseman, and a number of younger poets and novelists. I have written before (in *A.M. Klein*) that there is a sense in which the Jews are
the most Canadian of Canadians: history has forced them to experience the conflicts and tensions that all sensitive Canadians experience, but to an intense degree. The search for honor and for dignity
in a world in flames, the prophets searching for vision in the desert
of a new country: these themes are Jewish and Canadian and universal at once. Imaginative Zionism makes sense in a new country that
is gradually discovering itself. In a sense, Canada — even Montreal,
where so many of our Jewish writers grow up — can represent the
confused modern world in microcosm, as Hugh MacLennan suggests in *Return of the Sphinx*, because it is a coalition of minorities:
in this sense, an international country. The problem of identity is a
problem of the diversity of Canada and the world.

The Jewish writer, because of the degree and the dramatic history of his own "different-ness," can see (paradoxically) that every Canadian is a "Jew," a stranger; everyone lives behind the barriers of his own cultural past, though some attempt to see over them. Thus Atuk, the Eskimo poet, is employed to demonstrate Jewish bigotry to the Jew by displaying his own, like a mirror-image. Richler carries this insight further in *Cocksure* where the true Jew, in the eyes of the trendy modern world-at-large, is seen to be your average decent WASP Canadian, one Mortimer Griffin. But it is in *The Apprenticeship of Duddy Kravitz* that the Jew as Canadian, the Canadian as Jew, receives its most balanced, its funniest, and its most profound expression.

5 Ghost Writing:
Traces of Margaret Laurence

A matriarchal muse haunts some recent Canadian novels. As far as I can tell, nobody else has yet publically remarked upon the apparent homage to Margaret Laurence's *A Jest of God* that seems to have been (deliberately, I think, though I haven't asked) built into Margaret Atwood's *The Handmaid's Tale* as a kind of subtext.

Other books perhaps haunted by Margaret's ghost are Marian Engel's *Lunatic Villas* (published, of course, when both were still alive) and Timothy Findley's *Not Wanted on the Voyage*. All three authors were good friends of Margaret's and, for that matter, very well-disposed to one another. Indeed, Findley and Engel were close friends. And, for what it's worth, my judgment is that each of these novels happens to represent its highly distinctive and distinguished author at her or his best.

The Handmaid's Tale's first epigraph includes the same passage from Genesis that Laurence's text echoes:

> And when Rachel saw that she bare Jacob no children, Rachel envied her sister; and said unto Jacob, Give me children, or else I die.
>
> And Jacob's anger was kindled against Rachel; and he said, Am I in God's stead, who hath withheld from thee the fruit of the womb?
>
> — Genesis, 30: 1-2

"Nick —"

"Mm?"

"If I had a child, I would like it to be yours."

This seems so unforced that I feel he must see it the way I do. And so restrained, as well, when I might have torn at him — *Give me my children.*

His flesh, his skin, his bones, his blood — all are still connected with mine, but now suddenly not. Not a muscular withdrawal. Something different, something unsuspected.

His face turns away from mine. He puts his mouth momentarily on my shoulder. Then, still not looking at me, he brushes a hand across my forehead.

"Darling," he says, "I'm not God. I can't solve anything."

A Jest of God

The lover who may be the handmaid's savior is also called Nick. He is just as laconic and mysterious as Rachel's Nick. In each case the woman wants a child from the man. (And let us note in passing that the handmaid's lost husband is called Luke, a name that may have been borrowed from *The Fire-Dwellers*.) Blocked fertility and maternal deprivation figure largely in both books; and both Rachel and the handmaid have a likeable, wise-cracking, lesbian friend.

Of course, the two books are also very different. The story of an unhappy spinster schoolteacher in a small, old-fashioned Canadian town where little ever changes and a dystopian futuristic fantasy set near Harvard are two quite distinct animals — even if it is interesting to note that Atwood's ultra-puritanical society is even more rigid in its codes of behavior than Laurence's. But I believe that Atwood is paying homage to Laurence, at least in localized areas of her own novel.

Consider these two passages: the first from *A Jest of God*, the second from *The Handmaid's Tale.*

How can I have this lightness? It's temporary, a reaction. It won't last.

At that moment, when I stopped, my mind wasn't empty or paralysed. I had one clear and simple thought.

They will all go on in some how, all of them, but I will be dead as stone and it will be too late then to change my mind.

But nothing is changed now. Everything is no more possible than it was. Only one thing has changed — I'm left with it, with circumstances, whatever they may be. I can't cope, and I can't opt out. What will I do? What will become of me?

The floorboards are splintered here, where the rug doesn't reach, and their roughness makes me realize what I am doing. I don't know why I should be doing this. It is both ludicrous and senseless. I do not know what to say, or to whom. Yet I am on my knees.

I am not praying — if that is what I am doing — out of belief. Only out of need. Not faith, or belief, or the feeling of deserving anything. None of that seems to be so.

Help me.

Help — if You will — me. Whoever that may be. And whoever You are, or where. I am not clever. I am not as clever as I hiddenly thought I was. And I am not as stupid as I dreaded I might be. Were my apologies all a kind of monstrous self-pity? How many sores did I refuse to let heal?

We seem to have fought for a long time, I and You.

The ones who do not have anyone else, turn to You — don't you think I know? All the nuts and oddballs turn to You. Last resort. Don't you think I know?

My God, I know how suspect You are. I know how suspect I am.

If You have spoken, I am not aware of having heard. If You have a voice, it is not comprehensible to me. No omens. No burning bush, no pillar of sand by day or pillar of flame by night.

I don't know what I've done. I've been demented, probably. I know what I am going to do, though.

Look — it's my child, mine. And so I will have it. I will have it because I want it and because I cannot do anything else.

A Jest of God

I pray where I am, sitting by the window, looking out through the curtain at the empty garden. I don't even close my eyes. Out there or inside my head, it's an equal darkness. Or light.

My god. Who Art in the Kingdom of Heaven, which is within.

I wish you would tell me Your Name, the real one I mean. But *You* will do as well as anything.

I wish I knew what You were up to. But whatever it is, help me to get through it, please. Though maybe it's not Your doing; I don't believe for an instant that what's going on out there is what You meant.

I have enough daily bread, so I won't waste time on that. It isn't the main problem. The problem is getting it down without choking on it.

Now we come to forgiveness. Don't worry about forgiving me right now. There are more important things. For instance, keep the others safe, if they are safe. Don't let them suffer too much. If they have to die, let it be fast. You might even provide a Heaven for them. We need You for that. Hell we can make for ourselves.

I suppose I should say I forgive whoever did this, and whatever they're doing now. I'll try, but it isn't easy.

Temptation comes next. At the Centre, temptation was anything much more than eating and sleeping. Knowing was a temptation. What you don't know won't tempt you, Aunt Lydia used to say.

Maybe I don't really want to know what's going on. Maybe I'd rather not know. The Fall was a fall from innocence to knowledge.

I think about the chandelier too much, though it's gone now. But you could use a hook, in the closet. I've considered the possibilities. All you'd have to do, after attaching yourself, would be to lean your weight forward and not fight.

Deliver us from evil.

Then there's Kingdom, power, and glory. It takes a lot to believe in those right now. But I'll try it anyway. *In Hope,* as they say on the gravestones.

You must feel pretty ripped off. I guess it's not the first
time.
If I were You I'd be fed up. I'd really be sick of it. I guess
that's the difference between us.
I feel very unreal, talking to You like this. I feel as if I'm
talking to a wall. I wish You'd answer. I feel so alone.
All alone by the telephone. Except I can't use the
telephone. And if I could, who could I call?
Oh God. It's no joke. Oh God oh God. How can I keep on
living?

The Handmaid's Tale

Rachel prays after failing to commit suicide. The handmaid
(whose name may be June) also sends her variation on the Lord's
Prayer to a God whose nature she cannot fathom, and as an alternative to suicide. Both women look out an upper window. Each
monologue is dramatically effective to a high degree in its individual context. "Help me," says Rachel; "m'aidez," say the rebellious
handmaids to one another. And this is no jest. "God's pity on God"
inhabits both books.

Both books take us intimately into the mind of a first-person
female narrator. And behind *A Jest of God*, one feels, lies Sinclair
Ross's *As for Me and My House*, the diary of the otherwise nameless (and trapped, and barren) Mrs. Bentley; this is a book Laurence
described as "the only completely genuine novel I had ever read
about my own people, my own place, my own time." It's a distinguished line of succession; and still there are those commentators,
often come from other countries, who deny that there is any
Canadian literary tradition.

Lunatic Villas has two writers in its largeish cast of comic characters: the journalist Harriet Ross, who is the novel's central protagonist, and a profane, hard-drinking novelist with the ridiculous
name of Marshallene. Marshallene doesn't seem to me to resemble
at all the only female writer and friend of Marian Engel's named
Marshall that I am acquainted with, so I'll attach no special significance to the name. But both of these women are somewhat Lauren-
cian. Harriet is everybody's mother, almost a parody of the strongly

maternal Laurence heroine, and at least twice as harrassed as
Stacey in *The Fire-Dwellers*. Marshallene is big, vulgar, and brassy.
"Harriet's kids have two words for everything, gross and neat-o.
Marshallene is gross." She is credited by the excessively neat
Vinnie, who finds her distasteful as a woman, with writing a first-
rate novel about pioneers, Ontario pioneers as it happens, but one
thinks of *The Stone Angel* when he says "this is the only thing I've
read about my ancestors that isn't bullshit."

My subjective feeling is that Marshallene is a comic exaggeration of the "tough broad" side both of Margaret Laurence and of
Marian Engel herself. Both women projected an interesting combination of delicacy and earthiness in their best writing. And
Marshallene's toughness doesn't quite cover her vulnerability, as
her longest and most hilarious speech reveals. It also reveals the
personal cost that some very good female writers have paid for
their achievement, something both authors knew about from bitter experience.

The focal consciousness of much of *Not Wanted on the Voyage*
is Mrs. Noyes. Her defiance of a cruel, patriarchal God adds another variation on the prayer scenes quoted above:

> *But I will not pray: not to You gone mad up there with*
> *Your vengeance. I will never pray to You again. I will pray*
> *to anyone — to anything — I will pray . . .*
> To the river.
> Yes.
> *Dear River — please — allow me through to the other side.*
> *I crave your mercy and I beg your pardon — that I should*
> *trespass here. But there is a child — and the child is*
> *frightened of you — and she wants — she needs to be taken*
> *to the other side. And only I can take her — please — allow*
> *me to pass. . . . Amen.*
> *And — oh, yes — I beg your mercy, too, on these*
> *frightened creatures who travel with me.*

> *Not Wanted on the Voyage*

Mrs. Noyes believes in what Findley has called, in an interview in the first volume of Donald Cameron's *Conversations with Canadian Novelists*, "a being that is all of nature." Later she says that we should all pray to one another. She also prepares to die since she at first refuses to enter the ark and prefers to share the fate of the excluded creatures.

I am indebted to Heather Robertson for the suggestion that Mrs. Noyes resembles Margaret Laurence herself. True, it is gin she drinks in quantity, not Scotch, but her attitudes and habits may seem familiar to anyone who spent time with Margaret. And later, teaching the novel, I was struck by this description:

> There were ribbons round her neck and an apple in her hand — the apple half-eaten, the ribbons — of every colour — slowly melting into the patchwork of her shawls and aprons. In appearance, Mrs. Noyes had become a kind of walking flea-market: all her strips of petticoat and ribbon, rag and rope and sashes hanging down in front and behind; and all her pockets, plackets and dangling purses bulging with bits of string and jars of buttons, lace caps and clothes pins, needles, scissors, bags of medicinal herbs and books of pins. Rose petal *sachets* salvaged from the trousseau chest. ANY OLD ANYTHING! might have been her sign.

Is there here an echo of Hagar Shipley, disheveled by the sea in the latter part of *The Stone Angel*? An affectionate parody? Mrs. Noyes is not fierce and narrow like Hagar, of course; she is a rebel in the service of maternal, nurturing values. She holds a bear in her arms (an echo of Engel here?) and cherishes all life. If she is another of the older women in Findley's novels with "brooding . . . non-intellectual sensibility," as he described such characters in an interview in Graeme Gibson's *Eleven Canadian Novelists*, she is the most positive and life-affirming one.

A final, personal case. When I was writing *Adele at the End of the Day*, one of whose two central figures is a seventy-year-old woman reviewing her life, I was consciously fearful that my own reviewers might find her derivative of Hagar in *The Stone Angel*. In the event, nobody did, and I do think she is quite different. I told

myself that she was seventy, not ninety, one of two main characters, that she was a not very maternal Jewish mother, that she was
rich, that she lived in a Toronto hotel suite, and had lived her life
in Paris, London, and Rosedale. She was more traveled and sophisticated than Hagar, though not more intelligent or any less tart
and bitter. Most important, her voice is completely her own, not
an echo of any other character. (I've subsequently thought of some
real women who may have contributed to that particular voice,
though I wasn't conscious of them when I was writing.)

And yet. Could I have written an older woman from the inside
out, largely in the first person, without having previously read
with great admiration the novels of Margaret Laurence? I suspect
not. I'm not quite so possessed by my characters as she said she
was; I'm not a "method novelist." I don't think I'm either as emotional or as nervously intense as she was. But I have no doubt that
she is one of the important novelists, female and male, Canadian
and other, whose technique and vision have helped me. So if
Margaret's ghost is not actually *in* my second novel in the way
that she is (I feel) in the other books I've cited, she is certainly
standing just behind, looking over my shoulder as I write.

Moreover, I find that I too have written a sort of prayer-scene to
set beside those already quoted:

> Oh God. Where is that drink? I must have left it in the
> bathroom. Again.
>
> It makes life bearable. Gin. I don't know how I'd go on
> without it. It's probably keeping me alive. Now there's a
> thought for the good doctor. He thinks I have an occasional
> cocktail, and doesn't disapprove. He doesn't know (or
> doesn't want to know) I guzzle quantities each afternoon.
> Perhaps I'll die with glass in hand. That'll be a hoot.
>
> When I'm called up for judgement God will say, "Now
> what's this I hear of you. Drinking every day. Indulging in
> fornication on a vast scale till you got too old to be
> attractive any more. Tormenting my servant Florence in
> what should have been your gentle and serene golden years.
> Refusing your otherwise useless money to my most
> excellent and devoted servant Brother Gary. I'm afraid you

missed your one chance at salvation there, my girl. So it's off to the eternal fires with you. Sorry. 'Cause you're not a bad sort, otherwise. But I'm afraid that's how it adds up."
And I'll say, "Up Yours, Jehovah. I don't think so much of the job You've done either."
He only smiles. He's been saving His most devastating point for the last shaft.
"You were a lousy mother," He says.
"Damn You, God," I say.
Blasphemy. The nuns would faint. But no lightning strikes.
Once, of course, I did wonder, very seriously, who or what God might be. After the war I guess I gave up on Him. After we saw what we saw. I couldn't think any more about Him. And yet.
The world *is* beautiful. Still. The leaves on this tree-lined street are beautiful. Even this small hotel has an elegance that pleases me. Most of it. The angel-tree, my one poem, would seem to suggest that I can't really *shake* God. He lurks in my subconscious perhaps.

Adele at the End of the Day

This is certainly in the spirit of Margaret's struggling heroines. And perhaps I should point out the obvious here: that in none of the books mentioned is Christian fundamentalism very popular.

Of course, Margaret didn't write the kind of comedy that can be found in *Adele* and in *Lunatic Villas*. Nor did she write either a dystopian or an adult's beast fable with fairly overt political and social messages. But if she could take Catharine Parr Traill as a guardian angel, as Morag does in *The Diviners* (and I think Margaret was quite conscious that Margaret Atwood had already made Traill's sister Susanna Moodie a muse, later on remarking in a television film: "my muse is female and old"), then it is not surprising that Laurence herself should haunt the very disparate works of her successors even before her death. She had already become one of the ancestors.

6 Re-Visioning: Comedy and History in the Canadian Novel

Canadian comedy in English arises out of those Canadian cultural tensions that have been with us at least since the Loyalists. The European-American tension that engenders Canadian ambivalence and the "between worlds" theme can be found in T.C Haliburton's *Clockmaker*, in Susanna Moodie's *Roughing it in the Bush*, a fictionalized memoir which provides an archetypal pattern and structure for much later Canadian fiction, especially that by women, and in Stephen Leacock's ironic evocation both of the town that is Canada's past and the city that replaced it. Indeed, Haliburton, Moodie, and Leacock provide the beginnings of a significant Canadian fiction in their ability to make comedy out of cultural and psychological tensions; this paves the way for the shrewd social comedy of W.O. Mitchell, Mordecai Richler, Robertson Davies, Margaret Atwood, Marian Engel, Robert Kroetsch, Jack Hodgins, Leonard Cohen (in *Beautiful Losers*), and others. Canadian cultural uncertainty and ambivalence are the sources of Canadian comedy.

Judge Haliburton himself seems to have embodied the original Canadian tension. He once said: "I am Sam Slick, says I, at least what is left of me." He had roots in New England as well as old England. Though learned and respectable, he also loved bawdy jokes and, according to Ray Palmer Baker's 1924 introduction to *The Clockmaker*, the company of "hostlers and fishermen rank with the obscenities of the stable and the dory." He also loved the taproom and excelled in the art of telling unprintable stories. He seems to have been (not altogether unlike contemporary poet Al Purdy) an interesting mixture of roistering good fellow, on the one hand, and scholar and gentleman on the other — that is, he is the British squire and the Yankee pedlar combined. His two heroes reflect the British and American aspects, respectively, of his character.

Haliburton deplores American social disorder, and predicts the civil war. But he also supplies Sam Slick (towards whom he knows we will experience our usually profoundly mixed feelings about Americans and their doings) with an effective speech attacking the conceit and condescension of the Englishman visiting North America. As for his Nova Scotians, they are described as "a cross of English and Yankee, and therefore first cousins to us both." Their country is "like this night; beautiful to look at, but silent as the grave — still as death, asleep, becalmed." The people, Sam says, have not really engaged that sleeping monster, their physical environment. Nova Scotia is a happy backwater that could be rich as well if the people would develop their natural resources. A certain amount of American enterprise, then (but without the anarchy that often goes with that energy), would be beneficial.

Haliburton's politics are pragmatic and cautiously progressive conservative like Leacock's later on. The reformers of his time are characterized as misinformed and overcome with passion, but his own Tories are not spared, since Sam warns them of "the prejudices of birth and education" and remarks shrewdly that "power has a natural tendency to corpulency." In *The Clockmaker* one detects the ability to see two or more sides to every question, a pragmatic rather than a reactionary conservatism, an ability to live with uncertainties and antagonistic philosophies, an awareness of shifting perspectives. Thus Haliburton's Mr. Hopewell argues for a synthesis of the best qualities of British constitutional monarchy and American republicanism, that is, for a British system of government well adapted to North American conditions. This is the Canadian via media.

Haliburton expresses, then, the ambivalence of Canadian comedy: the things Canadian, American, and British that he admires or criticizes are inside him as well as outside him; one senses divided loyalties, ironic undertones like those in such later comic works as *Sunshine Sketches, The Apprenticeship of Duddy Kravitz,* or *A Mixture of Frailties.*

Susanna Moodie also develops the comedy of cultural tensions. For while the judge was telling his tales of the clockmaker pushing clocks on the timeless, this English gentlewoman was struggling for psychological survival in darkest Ontario. Here is a sentimental lady novelist and poet who was forced by circumstances beyond her control to look hard at Canada. The story she tells in *Roughing it in the Bush* is, like those later on of Sinclair Ross's Mrs. Bentley in *As for Me and My House,* Margaret Laurence's Hagar Shipley in *The Stone Angel,* Margaret Atwood's nameless heroine in *Surfacing,* or even Marian Engel's Lou in *Bear,* one of initiation, a kind of physical and moral odyssey of discovery. These works articulate the tension between pride and the spirit of place: a somewhat fictionalized, often humorous memoir is ancestor to significant (but not very humorous) later works of fiction.

Mrs. Moodie makes comedy of her encounters with her "Yankee" neighbors, presenting herself (just how consciously it is a little difficult to determine) as an officious, priggish, and more than faintly ridiculous snob:

> "Do you swear?"
> "Swear! What harm? It eases one's mind when one's vexed. Everybody swears in this country. My boys all swear like Sam Hill; and I used to swear mighty big oaths till about a month ago, when the Methody parson told me that if I did not leave it off I should go to a tarnation bad place; so I dropped some of the worst of them."
> "You would do wisely to drop the rest; women never swear in my country."
> "Well, you don't say! I always heer'd they were very ignorant. Will you lend me the tea?"

One might be forgiven for wondering whether this exchange took place exactly as it is recorded; in any case, I think old Betty Fye got the best of it. Having digested her difficult experience, Mrs. Moodie seems able, after years in the clearings of Belleville, to laugh at herself. She reveals all her contradictions, retaining her ingrained class attitudes and gentility but recognizing the necessity of change. In her account of her bush neighbors she retains her superiority by depicting her adversaries as amoral goons while admitting elsewhere that a spirit of friendly co-operation does exist in the backwoods. Somewhat grudgingly, she comes to see that society must be arranged differently in the new world and that this is for the best. In her consideration of the "servant problem," for example, she comes to the — to her — "astonishing realization" that the "homage to rank and education" displayed by the lower orders in England "is not sincere," and then proceeds to the conclusion that the relative independence of the Canadian working class is a healthy development. Like Haliburton, Mrs. Moodie inches in the direction of a more sophisticated and socially concerned conservatism. Thus Robin Mathews has, in *Canadian Literature: Surrender or Revolution*, aptly called her a "pink Tory."

I have written elsewhere in this book about the balanced structure of *Sunshine Sketches*, Leacock's minor masterpiece. Leacock's humor too is the humor of ambivalence. For he was always compromised as a social critic by his own membership in the privileged establishment (the Mausoleum Club), by the benefits and habits of wealth and status. An ironist, he will forgive in others that ambition and selfishness he can see in himself. This prevents him from developing any further than he did his tendency to a harsh Juvenalian or Swiftian satire. If human nature is ever thus, then no radical reform is possible; those who, like Tomlinson in *Arcadian Adventures with the Idle Rich* and the Mariposans, can live out their contradictions in a simpler environment, are fortunate. But Leacock himself is not always one of these. And the tendency of human civilization is toward increasing complexity in the city of the future — a belief that is potentially tragic unless one believes as well that human nature retains some generosity and imaginative resources even in circumstances of increasing complexity. Leacock, whose variable temperament involved both a genial appreciation of the goodness of the world and what his brother called a terrible despair, seems never to have quite resolved these issues.

For this reason he could not be, consistently, a satirist. Nor could he be a realist striving to present things "as they are"; he does not

seem to have been sure just how they were. Thus his multiple or
shifting perspective, a technique I have termed "Canadian" since it
can render the physical and psychological paradoxes and incon-
gruities, the complex fate, so to speak, that is Canada. At its best
this might be called myriad-mindedness.

Leacock greatly admired Mark Twain. So does W.O. Mitchell.
But the Mitchell of *Who Has Seen the Wind?* is finally more like
Leacock than he is like Twain. His town is a version of Mariposa
west. Though the outcast older Ben is a rascal not unlike Pap Finn
(who also pretends to repent) in *Huckleberry Finn*, he is treated a
good deal more sympathetically than the truly vicious old Finn,
since Mitchell is a kindly, tolerant observer, like Leacock; when
Ben is convicted for keeping a still by a judge who is one of his
best customers, it is reminiscent of the episode in *Sunshine
Sketches* in which Judge Pepperleigh fines Josh Smith because
Smith has closed the bar and left the judge outside without a
drink. Mitchell soft-pedals the meanness and hypocrisy of the
townspeople (though this is there — in the treatment of the
Chinese, of the outcast Bens and the crazed Saint Sammy) almost
as much as Leacock in order to preserve an essentially comic
vision. He even allows the town's malevolent social dictator, Mrs.
Abercrombie, to suffer defeat at the hands of the progressive young
schoolmarm. There are good, sensitive, and sympathetic people in
the town — two teachers, a doctor, a shoemaker, all of the boy
Brian's family — and this does much to offset the surrounding garrison atmosphere of repression and small-mindedness. Excessive
sentimentality is avoided, though only just: a fine balance is
achieved. Brian, Mitchell's focal consciousness, is basically a good
boy (like Tom Sawyer, but more genuinely imaginative), not a
rebel; the young Ben is wilder — more like Huck Finn. In determining to be a soil conservationist Brian brings the two worlds of
town and prairie together in good Canadian balance; he will never
light out for the unknown like an American hero. Town and physical environment, life and death, good and evil are balanced in
Mitchell's as in Leacock's comic vision.

Robertson Davies is similarly imbued with the spirit of Leacock.
Both his Salterton and his Deptford are populated by modern and
not-so-modern Mariposans. Davies deepens the vision of Leacock,

however, with his Jungian insights into human nature and growth; as a psychological novelist he can be compared to Morley Callaghan or Hugh MacLennan who are also interested in the ways in which good and evil, light and dark, are not strictly separable, since good often seems to result from evil, and vice versa. This is the morally ambivalent "world of wonders" in which the glory and the darkness go together, and even shade into one another. But the balance struck by Davies the comic artist is still Leacock's balance, informed by a concerned and tolerant conservatism.

I have argued elsewhere in this book that Mordecai Richler's comedy is similarly based, and that even in its very Jewishness it reflects the Canadian cultural tensions and anomalies: Richler's Montreal has the same cultural cross-currents, only more complex, as Haliburton's Nova Scotia, Moodie's backwoods, and Leacock's Mariposa. Equally sophisticated is Robert Kroetsch's comic probing of western Canadian identity in such novels as *The Studhorse Man, Gone Indian,* and *Badlands.* Kroetsch has observed, as Leacock might have (had he too been interviewed by Donald Cameron for his *Conversations with Canadian Novelists*), that Americans are interested in expansion and Canadians in equilibrium. In his own novels sex and death (sometimes bone and penis), poetry and criticism, life and art are held in balance. Then there is Jack Hodgins who mixes Garcia Marquez and Mariposa in his invention of a Vancouver Island town in *The Resurrection of Joseph Bourne.*

And there are other notable comic novels, to which the Leacock-Kroetsch principle may be applied: Matt Cohen's *The Sweet Second Summer of Kitty Malone,* another book about passages, stages of life, and town and country, Richard B. Wright's *The Weekend Man,* and Adele Wiseman's *Crackpot,* the comedy that balances her magnificent tragic action in *The Sacrifice,* are three that spring to mind. A fourth is Wright's *Farthing's Fortunes,* a marvelously entertaining re-creation of the basic British-American or "Canadian" tension defined so long ago by Haliburton.

No doubt the list could be lengthened. Ethel Wilson was a fine comic writer and shrewd observer of the peculiarities of a new society. Atwood's *The Edible Woman* is, I would argue, balanced and tolerant in Leacock's way. So is David Helwig's *A Sound Like Laughter.* (Atwood and Helwig are, of course, astringent if not bleak comedians. Both are poets in the novel, a matter I have dealt with elsewhere.) And the witty, warm, and sophisticated novels of Marian Engel, especially *The Honeymoon Festival* and *Lunatic Villas*, should not be overlooked. *Lunatic Villas* reveals the crazy social mixture of urban Canada as only Engel (or perhaps, working his own street, Mordecai Richler) can do, and it celebrates, as Canadian authors generally are wont to do, family and community, however eccentric the forms they take. In this case it is the inhabitants of a street in Toronto who constitute, in microcosm, the human comedy.

Canadian comedy, then, is generated by Canadians' acute awareness of complexity and uncertainly. But what about the equally acute Canadian longing for clearer definition and purpose? Here we touch upon the other and perhaps more important tradition of Canadian fiction.

This involves the novel as romance and the novel as history. It is arguable, for instance, that the three most ambitious novelists working in Canada in recent years are the equally historically-minded Hugh Hood, Rudy Wiebe, and Matt Cohen. And at least three others, Graeme Gibson, Timothy Findley, and Heather Robertson (with her lively *Willie* trilogy, one of those works in which Canadian comedy, romance, and history impressively converge), share the fascination with the past.

It is perhaps indicative of the present stage of our evolving literary culture that these writers and others have been engaged in what may be termed the "re-visioning" of Canadian history and character — that is, each attempts to reveal to Canadians a new or more "true" fictional version of our collective past. Each can thus be considered within the context of a tradition of moral (and often religious) historical fiction that includes such giants as Tolstoy, Thomas Mann, Solzhenitzyn, Faulkner, and D.H. Lawrence abroad, and such new ancestors as F.P. Grove, Hugh MacLennan, Margaret Laurence, and the Robertson Davies of *Fifth Business* and *Murther and Walking Spirits* at home. Both Wiebe and Cohen express admiration for the pioneering work of Grove even while evolving narrative methods and prose styles that remind one sometimes of Faulkner, sometimes of Lawrence; both Wiebe and Hood write from a deeply committed Christian perspective while disagreeing on important political and cultural matters. All see the novel as history, and would probably agree with D.H. Lawrence, as Hugh MacLennan does, that the novel occurs when the soul encounters history. Indeed, the project of historical re-visioning is shared by such important (and sometimes "epic") novels as *The Master of the Mill, The Watch That Ends the Night, Voices in Time, The Diviners, Fifth Business, Murther and Walking Spirits, Solomon Gursky Was Here, The New Age, The Disinherited, The Blue Mountains of China, The Temptations of Big Bear, The Scorched-Wood People, The Wars, Famous Last Words, Not Wanted on the Voyage, Perpetual Motion,* and *Willie.* And most of these concern themselves with Canadian history.

Historical romance was the alternative to comedy in nineteenth-century Canadian fiction. Romances and such romantic narrative poems as Isabella Valancy Crawford's *Malcolm's Katie* or, later on, E.J. Pratt's approximations of epic were perhaps more appropriate responses to the rugged new country than the well-developed novel of society, a form that had replaced and sometimes transformed (in order to preserve) the epic and the romance in Europe when the western kingdoms had reached a certain level of social, political, and economic sophistication. Don Quixote bade a reluctant farewell to the older, simpler order, but the celebration of physical struggle for survival and human dignity is necessarily revived in the new world, as much American and Canadian writing makes abundantly clear. Captain Ahab and E.J. Pratt's Brébeuf are like heroes out of epic or romance.

In any case, and for whatever reasons, the "realistic" social novel did not for a long time find many practitioners in Canada. *The Clockmaker* takes the form of a diary, and *Roughing It in the Bush* is a fictionalized memoir that can easily be seen as a romance of discovery. Both offer, as I have suggested, thematic and, as may be indicated by Sinclair Ross's diary-novel *As For Me and My House*, perhaps even formal clues to future novelists. In Mrs. Moodie's self-dramatization we see the beginning of a Canadian literary type — the sensitive artist faced with a hostile environment. Grove sounds this theme again, and Ross develops it further in the portrait of Mrs. Bentley and her husband. Ernest Buckler's *The*

Mountain and the Valley presents it as tragic romance.

The popular historical novels of Kirby and Richardson, modeled upon the historical novel as practiced by Sir Walter Scott, may represent an evasion of the contemporary scene; probably they reflect as well, though, that sense already mentioned, that romance and heroic adventure could express in symbolic and sometimes literal form the struggle with the new land. In the twentieth century such Canadian novelists as Thomas B. Costain and — on a much more accomplished plane — Thomas Raddall continue this tradition. (And, interestingly enough, Matt Cohen has attempted to revive the historical romance as a vehicle for serious historical insight in *The Spanish Doctor*. In this he is at least partly successful, though he has here eschewed his usual rural Canadian content. But as in A.M. Klein's *Second Scroll* one can see parallels between the Jewish quest for a new home and the Canadian search for community.)

Unfortunately, there was in the last century no *Scarlet Letter* or *Moby Dick* among the Canadian historical romances, that is, no book as insightful, or that has illuminated Canadian experience as profoundly or eloquently as Hawthorne did that of New England or Melville that of Western man falling victim to his North American hubris. It is true that Richardson's *Wacousta* — as interpreted by such readers as John Moss, Margot Northey, Michael Hurley, Gaile MacGregor, or Robin Mathews — may suggest the Canadian tension and search for balance between freedom and order, wilderness and garrison, but it is too sensational, crudely written, and clumsily constructed a work to bear much comparison with the more resonant fables of American identity. Our own masterworks come later.

Such popular regional romancers as L.M. Montgomery and Mazo de la Roche perhaps provide — like Leacock, in his own way — bridges to a more "realistic" fiction. But only Sara Jeannette Duncan is able, at the turn of the century, to write a realistic social novel, *The Imperialist*, about a small Ontario town. (It contains, incidentally, an acute awareness of the comedy of cultural tensions.) "Realism" arrives in earnest only in the 1920s with Frederick Philip Grove and Morley Callaghan.

Even Grove, however, turns to historical allegory in *The Master of the Mill*. And there are strong elements of romance in *The Mountain and the Valley* and in even the most "realistic" novels of Callaghan, MacLennan, Ross, Laurence, and others. Certain figures, themes, and images — most if not all common to our Western heritage — are rearranged in a pattern that may be styled "Canadian," as Northrop Frye, D.G. Jones, and others have attempted to show. In *A Time for Judas* even Callaghan has, like Matt Cohen, returned to the historical novel.

Grove's vision is "epic" in its cultivation of the "long view." Of his nature essays he wrote: "I wanted the simpler, the more elemental things, things cosmic in their associations, nearer to the beginning or end of creation." Most Canadian writers of importance have, it seems, cultivated in prose or poetry this "long view." Both pre-history and the end of all civilization can seem close in the open spaces.

In his best novels, *Settlers of the Marsh* and the no doubt autobiographical *A Search for America*, Grove presents European man struggling with a new environment that threatens to destroy his finer values even as it forces him to throw aside the inessential affectations of the old world. Grove here makes a kind of epic of the struggle with environment, and in *The Master of the Mill*, a much clumsier work, an allegory of the further struggle with the machine-as-environment. His work reflects, then, the period of Canada's relatively swift passage from pioneer society to sophisticated technological society. In this period the machine threatens to become the environment, and the anxieties this causes may be felt as strongly in the work of Grove (and that of his poetic counterpart Pratt) in Canada as in that of D.H. Lawrence in his English mining country. Grove's mill can symbolize either liberation from want or the tyranny of mechanism: the novel has a kind of ambivalent double-vision. It presents the social and political history of the early twentieth century in terms of the lives of one family.

Grove is, in English anyhow, usually a rather clumsy stylist. But he left behind his courageous personal example of heroic struggle and his insights into the nature of western Canadian life and European man's encounter with the new world to inform the finer talents and western sensibilities of Sinclair Ross, W.O. Mitchell, Margaret Laurence, and Ruby Wiebe. Wiebe's first novel,

Peace Shall Destroy Many, is reminiscent in a number of ways of *Settlers of the Marsh*. And Matt Cohen has said to me that he considers *A Search for America* "a great book." Interestingly enough, Cohen's own major novel *The Disinherited* employs Grove's framework of the conflict between fathers and sons on the land, and presents a version of the history of the new world as it may be seen in the lives of one family, and with a technical sophistication that Grove the novelist did not possess.

But between Grove and the historical novels of the 1960s and afterwards come those works — especially those by Callaghan, Ross, and Buckler — which offer studies in the frustration or even destruction of the artist or religious and moral visionary in the new world. This certainly reflects a phase of Canadian cultural development, the one expressed in poetry by A.M. Klein's "Portrait of the Poet as Landscape." The most important novels of this kind are *Such is My Beloved*, *The Loved and the Lost*, *As for Me and My House*, and *The Mountain and the Valley*. The last two are, in my opinion (along with *The Stone Angel* and *The Sacrifice*), among the few most powerful and most perfectly executed of Canadian novels. Both have important historical contexts without being historical fiction in quite the same explicit way that MacLennan's novels or *The Diviners* are.

The Mountain and the Valley is Canada's tragic romance, in which David Canaan, the artist or Moses-figure who has the potential to articulate the life of his family and community (in a verbal pattern analogous to the pattern of concentric circles in his grandmother's rug) and thus to enter the promised land of community, is obviously *chosen*, but chosen, it seems, to fail, to be sacrificed to the new country (as Isaac, another biblical type, is in *The Sacrifice*). But it is notable, of course, that where David fails, Buckler himself succeeds; the novel contains its tragic action, its linear narrative of the disintegration of a family, within a pattern of recurrent symbolic motifs — the mountain, the valley, the rug, the water, the sailor, the hermit, the tree of man and of life — that is circular, like the rug, as the story begins and ends on the same day.

It is novelists MacLennan, Laurence, and Wiseman (in Moses, the third generation in *The Sacrifice*, and in the indomitable Hoda of *Crackpot*) who move beyond the theme of the doomed visionary

to investigate the promised land itself. MacLennan seems to have
set out quite consciously, from *Barometer Rising* on, to articulate
the collective Canadian consciousness as it develops in the minds
and through the basic conflicts of his characters. A recurrent
metaphor in his work is the "explosion" that clears away the old
and allows new growth. The development of Canada is also drama-
tized, as many have observed, in terms of the struggles or love-hate
relationships between fathers (or tyrannical step-fathers or spiritual
fathers of various kinds) and sons. One observes the effects of literal and spiritual orphanhood, as in *As for Me and My House*. In
Barometer Rising and *Two Solitudes* the author is unequivocally
on the side of the new generation; by *Return of the Sphinx* he is
sympathizing deeply with the father. In *The Watch That Ends the
Night*, his most powerful and resonant novel, the "son" benefits
from the lessons of his spiritual father. A quest for maturity is completed in this epic romance. The near-mythic hero Jerome Martel
embodies (among other things) wild elemental Canada; George
Stewart represents a slowly-maturing social Canada that may be
instructed and revivified by contact with this native energy. Here a
kind of balance is found, only to be lost in the subsequent novel,
but perhaps regained in *Voices in Time*, in which it appears that
the lessons of the past are only temporarily forgotten. MacLennan
has moved in his seven novels from the explosion that supposedly
brought Canada to greater maturity in the First World War through
the explosion that destroyed Nazi Germany to the possible future
explosion that destroys for a time western industrial civilization.
At the conclusion of *Voices in Time* the future is once again in the
hands of the young. This is decidedly the novel as history, as in
Tolstoy. Indeed, MacLennan might be regarded as our Tolstoy, as
Callaghan is perhaps our Dostoievsky — each on a considerably
reduced scale.

Adele Wiseman's "crackpot" Hoda is said to occupy her past
and to inhabit her life: this is the "national" import that
Wiseman's two important novels share with those of her somewhat
more prolific friend Margaret Laurence. Both use the framework of
the entry into the promised land (as does, more ironically, the
Richler of *Duddy Kravitz*). In *The Stone Angel* and *The Diviners*
Laurence illuminates Canada's psychological history even more

searchingly than MacLennan did — partly because of the appropriateness to Canadian experience of the female perspective (the relevance of which MacLennan too had perceived in *The Precipice*, which chronicles Canada's difficult "marriage" with the United States).

The failure of Hagar Shipley's marriage is the failure of our ancestors to achieve a creative synthesis between old-world pride and the native energies of place. But in *The Diviners* the Currie plaid pin and the Métis knife are Pique's mixed inheritance, and her chances of succeeding where Hagar failed seem good. Pique is French, Indian, and Scottish combined. And her mother Morag is an artist or diviner, a mythmaker (like Al Purdy, who gives the novel its epigraph) who succeeds where David Canaan failed.

The Diviners has an allegorical dimension rather like that of one of MacLennan's earlier novels. Pique's role as reconciler of the dispossessed Scots, French, and Indian peoples resembles that of Paul Tallard in *Two Solitudes*. And Morag's three important men are each representative: Brooke (British imperialism as well as sexism), Dan (the Scottish past and heritage, the dispossession of the crofters, which he paints), and Jules (the native French-Indian, the experience of conquest). Each gives Morag (Canada) something though none can permanently be her lover. Jules, the dark, mysterious, non-WASP lover — successor in this role to Ukrainian Nick and Italian Luke of Laurence's two previous novels — is the most important. And it is interesting to note that the Tonneres, only mentioned and never directly encountered by the reader in *The Stone Angel*, are increasingly present in *The Fire-Dwellers* and *A Bird in the House*, and extremely important to the "national" theme of *The Diviners*.

In *The Diviners* the symbolic river of life and of time flows both ways, as it does in the mind of the artist-historian, or of God. To divine water is symbolically to discover and appreciate without resolving the mystery of life. When Morag and Royland observe a great blue heron in silence and "awe," the novel touches on the religious dimension, a context larger than the social, political, and historical. As in that other epic, *The Watch That Ends the Night*, all depends finally on grace, and everything ends in mystery. All that the various diviners of the novel can do, as the songs of Jules

and Pique make clear, is to memorialize and to that extent resur-
rect the dead, and thereby seek out individual and communal identity ("The valley and the mountain hold my name": the echo here
of Buckler's symbolism is surely deliberate). This is what, in all
her books, Laurence the orphaned diviner has done for herself and
for us.

Robertson Davies, Hugh Hood, Rudy Wiebe, Matt Cohen,
Timothy Findley, Graeme Gibson, Heather Robertson, and even
Alice Munro and Mavis Gallant (in their shorter fictions) are diviners too. Davies' great theme is the awakening of the Canadian
imagination: his Monica Gall and Dunstan Ramsay are psychic
torch-bearers, explorers of what Davies has called our "bizarre and
passionate life." And Hugh Hood has said that he wishes to capture
"the thoughts and textures of a century of Canadian life." He is,
like MacLennan before him and Heather Robertson later, the historian of the present century while Wiebe, Cohen, and Gibson look
to the further past for illumination.

The first six volumes of *The New Age,* Hood's projected twelve-
part epic of Canadian experience are *The Swing in the Garden, A
New Athens, Reservoir Ravine, Black and White Keys, The Scenic
Art,* and *The Motor Boys in Ottawa.* As his narrator Matthew
Goderich perceives more and more of life beyond infancy, so does
Canada, Hood suggests, as he conducts us through the 1930s,
1950s, 1920s, 1940s, and 1960s, dwelling in Canadian fashion on
trains, cars, boats, systems of communication, and even the communion of the living and the dead, all that binds us together, moving backwards and forwards with Matt's memories and re-lived
numinous moments.

In *Reservoir Ravine* a character who resembles the young Lester
Pearson declares: "I say to you that the Holy Land is in Manitoba
and in Québec, and it is the other way around too." In Hood's
Christian vision the human community as a whole strives toward
the new Jerusalem, and "Human history requires a double mode of
existence, an eternal state prior to temporal being, and that eternal
bliss reintegrated through time." In *Black and White Keys,* the
somewhat MacLennanesque book in which he takes on the Holocaust, Hood observes (as if he has perhaps been reading Northrop
Frye): "Bible history, the narrative of the pilgrimage of the Jews in

search of their homeland, was the great human exemplar of the search for home, one's place, a search that Andrew at last came to understand as the central task of his own people." Andrew Goderich, Matt's philosopher-father, exhorts Canadians (and the world) to create "the new state, the first modern society, the pacific country." This is the Canadian Zion again.

Another Christian, Ruby Wiebe, is also both historian and visionary, his particular business the re-visioning of the Canadian west — the territory opened up by Grove, Ross, and Laurence. *The Scorched-Wood People*, for instance, re-creates Riel and a rather generous interpretation of his visions. And in *The Temptations of Big Bear*, Wiebe's most impressive novel to date, each and every character is a real historical personage. Big Bear himself is a shaman or diviner whose visions foretell that destruction of his people's way of life that he is powerless to prevent. Big Bear is a tragic hero, even an unwitting type of Christ, as the title intimates. He resists the temptations to despair or to embrace violence, and he eventually lies down to die in dignity. But before he does there is a moment of magical communion with the captive white girl Kitty Mclean when the naked girl allows the sun to warm her and join her to the natural world, all the while watching the old man dance and hearing him chant, and then listening to his legends. He tells her that rock is the "grandfather of all, the first of all being as well as the last," and he will himself eventually join the land, as David Canaan also does, to be "changed continually into indistinguishable, as it seemed, and everlasting, unchanging rock." The brief communion of Indian shaman and white girl is the only incident that offers us hope that the holistic Indian vision of the world might persist and even flourish in our present lives in the way that John Newlove has suggested in his poem "The Pride." But the novel itself, a magnificent re-creation or "unearthing" of the tastes, smells, colors, touch, and texture of the Indian world, is an evidence and affirmation of that possibility.

Matt Cohen places the action of *The Disinherited* within the vast context of the long history of human disinheritance in the world; like Grove and Laurence and Wiebe, he considers our estrangement from the earth. His visionary poet writes a diary as he crosses the Atlantic to North America:

> We had thought ourselves better than our nomad ancestors
> who had wandered to Europe from Mesopotamia & Africa,
> but now we too were disinherited & forced to seek out a new
> world; & so we closed the circle on our past.

Closing the circle on the past, disinherited once more: this seems
to be what has happened to Erik Thomas too, after three generations of Thomases on the Ontario earth. Reading the poet's diary
Erik ought to be able to see parallels with his own experience. But
it remains unclear whether he learns the lesson of the poet's story.
The poet tells a tale that the ship's captain told him, of a magical
woman who bewitched him and cut off two of his fingers before
she would make love, but then, when the spell was broken,
seemed to be nothing but a fat whore after all. The lesson would
seem to be that even if the world is only a treacherous and dangerous whore, "fat and used," one must engage her and take the risk
involved or live in a void, a nothingness.

The onset of the modern technological world is a paramount
theme here as it was in Grove. And this has been a concern of
Graeme Gibson and Timothy Findley too. In *Perpetual Motion*
Gibson expresses it in terms of his nineteenth-century hero's obsession with a perpetual-motion machine. As the climax of the novel
approaches, a minor character remarks: "What strange intoxications
befall us as we rush with unprecedented speed into our restless and
striving future? The masses applaud. They must applaud the victory
of our dynamics, the triumph of Mind . . ." The complementary
theme — shared with Margaret Atwood, Michael Ondaatje, and a
number of other writers — of the war between man and the natural
world is seen in this novel in the mass slaughter of the pigeons. In
The Wars, Findley's powerful novel of Canadian initiation in the
First World War, the victimized rabbits and horses serve a similar
function. And *Not Wanted on the Voyage*, Findley's most impressive performance, amplifies this theme of man's mechanistic assault
on nature and the animals with its Blakean re-visioning of received
patriarchal myth to make it feminist and ecology-conscious. Like
Grove, MacLennan, Laurence, Hood, Wiebe, and Cohen, Gibson and
Findley attempt to tell us, through their historical re-visioning, how
we got the way we are.

So — in another way — does Heather Robertson in *Willie*. Here the effect of the First War on the growth of Canadian consciousness is treated both seriously and comically in terms of Robertson's trinity of Canadian types: romantic Talbot Papineau, neurotic and driven Willie King, and shrewd, sprightly Lily Coolican. Lily's dry and delightful wit is a welcome change from some of the more sombre fictional representatives of the Canadian soul that have suffered through earlier novels (for example, MacLennan's analogous Canadian trinity of Jerome, Catherine, and George in *The Watch That Ends the Night*). Here comedy, romance, and history are triumphantly reunited. But it is perhaps as well to remind oneself at this point that each "historical" novel that I have mentioned has its own unique combination of effects and qualities, its own formal structure and language. And each could, of course, be examined in and for itself in greater detail.

There is a sense, too, in which all fiction is historical. Fiction involves reflection on experience (whether personal or not). It involves knowledge and memory (whether personal or not). Memory, we discover, is itself selective, and is thus a primary form of fiction. History itself is a form of fiction, and fiction is history. This can be seen most purely, I think, in the work of such short-story writers as Alice Munro, Mavis Gallant, Joyce Marshall, and Clark Blaise. Munro's alter ego Del Jordan in *Lives of Girls and Women*, for instance, wants to render in words "every last thing" about her place and past. And Mavis Gallant's work displays a dominant personal-historical concern for the ways in which human beings are disillusioned, bereft of love, after childhood, and also disillusioned and disoriented, usually in Europe, after the Second World War.

But the major concern of this essay has been the more specifically "historical" re-visioning of Canada that has engaged most of our otherwise quite disparate major (and sometimes lesser) novelists. For it seems that when Canada is not perceived as comic and confused (that is, as Mariposa) it is often still perceived — as it was by Grove and MacLennan — as an epic quest or journey. It is sometimes — as in Gibson's and Findley's books — a misguided quest, but is nevertheless one that indicates, either negatively or positively, the necessity of finding integrity, self-understanding, and community. Perhaps it will be a sign that we have achieved or transcended these goals when the tradition of historical re-visioning has clearly exhausted itself.

Acknowledgements

Earlier versions of some of these essays have appeared in the following journals and/or critical anthologies. *A.M. Klein* (ed. Tom Marshall), *Beginnings* (ed. John Moss), *Canadian Literature*, *Cross-Canada Writer's Quarterly*, *Here and Now* (ed. John Moss), *Jewish Dialog*, *Modern Canadian Fiction* (ed. Carole Gerson), *Poetry Canada Review*, *Queen's Quarterly*, *Quiet Voices* (ed. Roger Bainbridge), *Spider Blues* (ed. Sam Solecki), *University of Windsor Review*, and *The Whig-Standard Magazine*.

The reviews included in Part One were originally published in the following magazines: *Books in Canada*, *Canadian Forum*, *Essays on Canadian Writing*, *The FM Guide*, *Ontario Review*, *Poetry Canada Review*, *Quarry*, *Queen's Quarterly*, and *The Whig-Standard Magazine*.

Index of Names

Ted Hughes 77, 80
Michael Hurley 113, 180

Henry James 112
Samuel Johnson
D.G. Jones 37, 61, 80, 81, 181
James Joyce 40, 114
Carl G. Jung 100,177

Franz Kafka 39, 41
John Keats 67
Penn Kemp 103
Leo Kennedy 37
William Lyon Mackenzie King
 49, 50, 54, 156
William Kirby 180
A.M. Klein 16, 22-42, 50, 55, 63,
 67, 71, 79, 120, 152, 153, 154,
 156, 160, 161, 180, 182
Raymond Knister 79
Joy Kogawa 116
Robert Kroetsch 172, 177

Archibald Lampman 55, 79
Red Lane 79
Margaret Laurence 35, 114, 156,
 161, 163-72, 174, 178, 179,
 181, 182, 183-84, 185, 186, 187
Wilfrid Laurier 156
D.H. Lawrence 17, 56, 70, 77,
 83, 114, 178, 181
T.E. Lawrence 97, 99, 100, 102,
 105, 106
Aviva Layton 58-59
Irving Layton 16-17, 34, 35, 37,
 38, 39, 40, 46, 50, 55, 58-64,
 79, 152, 161

Stephen Leacock 33, 34, 35, 113,
 118-130, 131, 136, 152, 153,
 159, 172, 175-76, 177, 180
Dennis Lee 65, 66, 88
Douglas Le Pan 116
David Lewis 37, 152
Gordon Lightfoot 44
Charles Lindbergh 44
Dorothy Livesay 37, 40, 54, 79
Yury Lotman 19
Robert Lowell 79
Pat Lowther 79
Jack Ludwig 39
Isaac Luria 23

John A. Macdonald 156
Gwendolyn MacEwen 9, 17, 66,
 89, 97-107, 116, 117
Stuart MacKinnon 37
Gaile MacGregor 180
Hugh MacLennan 113, 114, 151,
 161, 177, 178, 179, 181, 182,
 183, 184, 187, 188
Jay Macpherson 62, 82
Norman Mailer 146
Eli Mandel 39
Thomas Mann 178
Jacques Maritain 132, 146, 150
Joyce Marshall 41, 188
Gabriel Garcia Marquez 177
Karl Marx 150
Robin Mathews 175, 180
Seymour Mayne 36-37, 58
Meton 83
Herman Melville 179
Michelangelo 25, 30, 31
John Milton 20
Joni Mitchell 78